SHAPING THE
TEACHER
IDENTITY

8 Lessons That Will
Help Define the Teacher in You

SHAPING THE
TEACHER
IDENTITY

Kwame Sarfo-Mensah

SHAPING THE TEACHER IDENTITY
Eight Lessons That Will Help Define the Teacher in You

Kwame Sarfo-Mensah

ISBN: 1723480835

ISBN-13: 9781723480836

TABLE OF CONTENTS

$\mathcal{I}$NTRODUCTION

In the world of education, the most productive teachers pride themselves on their special ability to positively impact the impressionable minds of their students. They are able to justify their value through their students' standardized test scores and other forms of data. Indeed, these are legitimate ways to measure a teacher's impact in the classroom but they don't tell the full story. There is something to be said about the specific attributes a teacher possesses in order to be effective in the classroom. What are those intangible qualities that define the success of that teacher? The response to that question will consequently lead to an even deeper question -- how did that teacher acquire and develop these special qualities? That question can best be answered by exploring the source of their teacher identity.

Through this exploration, one will discover that the teacher's identity is directly and indirectly shaped by their unique life experiences and the valuable lessons they have learned from them. That being said, I believe that God placed certain people in my life to help shape me into the educator I am today. I can point to particular moments in my life that have tested my will, questioned my purpose, and solidified the fact that I was destined to be a role model for young children. In this book, I will take you through my personal journey and detail the many people, places, and situations that have provided me with valuable lessons that continue to guide my teaching career to this very day.

This book is, by no means, a step-by-step algorithm on how to become a teacher. I am simply sharing my truth with the hope that you, the reader, will be empowered in your personal quest to shape your teacher identity. This book is not solely intended for the aspiring educator. It is also intended for the seasoned educator who is at an emotional crossroads in their career and needs that source of inspiration that will reinvigorate their passion for teaching. If you are that educator, I hope my book will serve that purpose for you.

The process of developing a teacher identity is one that is evolutionary. For certain teachers, that process may take 5, 10 or more years before they are fully secure in who they are in the classroom. I personally can attest to this notion. Even with all the personal achievements, I've had in a career that has spanned 12 years in the classroom (the last 8 as a lead teacher), I am still a work-in-progress. I still feel that my best teaching years are just around the corner.

Each chapter in this book has a lesson for developing your teaching identity. Each lesson will cover the specific concept; provide an example from my experience, a summary, and the insights of another educator on the topic. This book is designed to spark ideas for the creation of your own teacher identity. As you read along, keep asking yourself:

- *How have my experiences guided my journey to becoming a teacher?*
- *What valuable lessons have I learned from those experiences?*

Let your own answers and the lessons in this book guide you into being the best teacher you can be.

My First Teacher

THROUGHOUT MY CAREER, I have had the privilege of teaching many young men in my classroom, many of whom came from households where a father figure was absent from their lives. In most of those situations, the mother was the sole caretaker in the home. I have always had a special affinity for mothers. Perhaps, it is because I am fortunate to have been raised by a wonderful woman for a mother.

A woman who migrated from her native Ghana in pursuit of a better life for her family in America. A woman who got all three of her children through college all while working the graveyard shift at a bank where she earned an annual salary of approximately $29,000. A woman whose unwavering optimism always shined through in the midst of personal adversity. A woman who has spent her entire life prioritizing the personal welfare of others even at the expense of her own. That woman is my mother, Dorothy A. Mensah. A chapter isn't enough to fully explain how my mother factors into my teacher identity equation. Quite frankly, she deserves her own book but I will surely do my very best to capture my mother's influence in my life.

I guess the best place to start this story will be June 1st, 1983, the official day my mother brought me into this Earth. Around this time, she had already given birth to my older brother, Sarfo, five years earlier and my father had already completed his MBA program at Western New England College (now called Western New England University). We resided in a small family home on 112 Hermitage Drive in Springfield, MA. Since I lived in Springfield for only a couple of years, I don't really have any memories about my time there. For me, my life really started when our family moved to Bloomfield, CT in the mid '80's.

Our new home was a two-story single-family property located on 239 Woodland Ave. Although Bloomfield was a predominantly Black middle-class suburban area, our neighborhood was a melting pot of diverse racial and cultural backgrounds. My mother started a new job at Fleet Bank, which is now called Bank of America. She worked the graveyard shift which started at around 11pm and ended around 7am the next morning. Her work schedule allowed her to spend time with us during the day and take care of her household duties. It was the perfect arrangement because my father worked at Aetna as an actuary during the day, which allowed our family to survive off two working incomes.

By all accounts, my parents were living the American dream. They arrived in this country as West African immigrants searching for a better life and successfully built our family from the ground up. Owning a home and raising three healthy children in a relatively safe suburban town served as convincing evidence of their triumph. My father was the breadwinner of the family but my mother was, and still is, unequivocally the heart and soul of the family.

For many of my fondest childhood memories, my mother was at the very center of them. When I think about my behavior management style and my overall demeanor when I interact with my students, all of that comes from my mother. I am undoubtedly the living embodiment of my mother. Her calm assertive approach to parenting is, in many ways, something that I have incorporated into my teaching philosophy. While my father was the hot-tempered disciplinarian who peppered his lectures with occasional personal insults and did most of his communicating with his belt, my mother served as the antithesis.

Her parenting style revolved around the concept of non-violence. She was not a proponent of spanking or any form of physical harm as a means of correcting behavior. Her recipe for effective parenting comprised of persistent nurturing and love. She never let a day go by without letting us know how much she loved and valued us. It was manifested through her delicious cooking and her corny jokes. It was manifested in the way that she affectionately smiled every time I arrived home from school. Most importantly, it was manifested in the respectful way she addressed me when I had a misstep with my behavior. In every scenario, I always knew that my mother was my biggest fan and number one advocate. This was most evident when I was going through my academic struggles in school.

During the first four grades of my schooling, I received special education services because of my difficulties with speech articulation. Even though I was a pretty smart kid, my inability to speak articulately hindered my ability to perform at the highest level academically. Most of the time, I knew what I wanted to say but, for some reason, there was a cognitive disconnect. My thoughts made sense in my mind but sounded nonsensical when they exited my mouth.

During those difficult years, my mother was a proactive participant of my special education process. At home, she made it a point to create vocabulary flash cards and sit down with me to help me practice my speech. She also gave me the job of reading to my little sister, Abena. My incentive for doing that job was two-fold. I earned a dollar every time I read to her and, more importantly, reading on a daily basis gave me additional practice with my speech. She was a consistent attendee at my Individual Education Plan (IEP) meetings, sharing with my teachers the different activities she did at home to help me with my speech issues. She even had my teachers asking her for advice on what they should do in the classroom to better facilitate my learning process. My mom wasn't a teacher by trade but her academic interventions at home were, at the very least, equally as effective as the ones my teachers did in school.

In hindsight, I truly believe that my mother's heavy involvement with my education expedited my learning process and made it possible for me to smoothly make the transition to the general education classroom at an earlier time than anticipated. When I think about the many mothers I have encountered throughout my teaching career, it troubles me that so many of them are not as informed about the special education process as my mother was. Too often have I seen mothers show up for the meetings just to sign the dotted line of their child's IEP. The special education coordinator is going through each section of the IEP with the mothers but they are using educational jargon that is way over their heads.

In those situations, I sometimes have to intervene to translate what the coordinator is saying in layman's terms so that they are fully aware of what academic supports the school is providing for their child. In my experience, many parents will nod their head in agreement with whatever information they are told but never take the time to thoroughly review the IEP and ask thoughtful questions to gain clarity around specific details they find confusing.

In general, parents, especially mothers, genuinely want to be actively involved in their children's education in any way they can but sometimes, their own insecurities can get in the way of them being active participants in their children's learning process. My mother never proclaimed to be an education expert but she did take the time to listen to my teachers and do her own research on learning strategies that she could do at home to help me become a better reader and communicator.

When my sister and I moved to Ghana with my father in 1995, I was overcome with emotion for many reasons. Besides the fact that I was leaving behind my friends in Bloomfield, I was going to be separated from the one individual who had always been my biggest fan and supporter in life. Being away from my mother for three years was easily one of the toughest experiences I went through in my life. My father tried to fill the void but it just wasn't the same feeling. Quite frankly, my father was never one to possess the "soft skills" gene. As much as I wanted to open up to him about my feelings and deepest thoughts, it was difficult for me to do so because I was fearful of him and he was not the most approachable person when it came to matters of the heart.

Thankfully, I had aunts and uncles who supported me and helped to make my transition to Ghana a smoother process but even they couldn't fully replace my mother. When my sister and I returned to the United States in 1998, it was the greatest feeling because we were reuniting with my mother and older brother. Even though her and my father were still legally married, their interactions with one another said otherwise. My mother was essentially playing the role of the single parent and doing everything in her power to keep the family afloat financially. She still had her overnight job at Bank of Boston (now called Bank of America) but that alone was not nearly enough to cover the monthly expenses.

In an effort to supplement her income, she picked up part-time jobs to do during the day. Some of those jobs included organizing books at a local library and working as a nanny for senior citizens. No matter how hard she worked, it seemed like the bills and expenses kept piling up. Personally, it never appeared that we were digging ourselves out of the financial hole. Everything felt like a huge struggle. In the midst of everything, my mother's faith in God never wavered as she was a deeply religious individual. Her number one priority was making sure that her children were happy and enjoying their lives.

Her unwavering sense of optimism brought about a sense of calm that assured us that we could overcome any obstacles that came in our path. At that time, I knew that my mother was going through a difficult time financially. On top of the monthly living expenses, she was paying tuition for my sister to attend the Greater Hartford Academy of Arts after school to study music theory. My older brother was still finishing up his undergraduate degree at Rensselaer Polytechnic Institute (RPI), which meant she was receiving an additional tuition bill to pay.

When money was really scarce, I could remember her making long distance phone calls to my father, asking him to transfer money to her bank account from Ghana. More often than not, my parents would end up arguing with each other about money. My father was in a good place financially and had the means to provide financial relief to our family but, for whatever reason, he had convinced himself to believe that my mother was lying about her financial struggles. Sadly, this pattern of behavior would persist throughout my high school tenure and continue during my college years. When I was struggling to pay my tuition at Temple, I remember calling my mother to see if she could send me money.

Given the fact that she was practically shouldering the financial burden for our family, she didn't always have the money available to me. She was responsible for all the family expenses: credit card debt, rent, utilities, car and health insurance, and my sister's school fees. When she didn't have the money, she would ask me to personally contact my father for it. So then I reached out to him about the money.

He then asked me if it was my mother's idea to ask him for money. If I had told him the truth, he would have automatically assumed that she was trying to pull a fast one on him. Believe it or not, I had to lie to my own father in order for him to help me pay my tuition so I could register for my new classes. It was one of the rare times during my five years of undergraduate study at Temple that my father contributed financially to my education.

Amazingly, my mother fully funded my education during that time frame and she accomplished that with a bank job that earned her an annual income that was approximately $29,000. To this day, I don't know how she was able to pull that off. All I know is that she made it happen and my bachelor's degree serves as a testament to her commitment of keeping me in school. Additionally, she covered my monthly rent during the three years I lived in my off-campus apartment in the heart of North Philly. Most students who were in a similar financial situation would have had to pick up a full-time job in order to pay for their tuition and cover their monthly rent. Fortunately, my mother never allowed me to go that route because she wanted all my energy to be focused on my academics.

This is exactly who Dorothy A. Mensah is. She is a woman who has been blessed with a humble heart and a natural gift for enhancing the quality of lives of those who are closest to her. Her life has been defined by the many personal sacrifices she has made for myself and my other siblings. Before she became a mother, she had aspirations of following the footsteps of her mother, Elizabeth Asare, and becoming a registered nurse. While my father was able to fulfill his dreams and embark on a successful career as an actuary, my mother's career had to take a backseat in order to become a full-time mother. She will never acknowledge this publicly but I know, in her heart, that she wished she could turn back the hands of time and have the opportunity to pursue her dreams.

Although being a devoted mother has, by far, been the greatest achievement in her life, I know, for a fact, that she envisioned a life so much greater than how it actually turned out. I can remember one conversation we had a few years back when she expressed her desire of starting a day care program in Ghana. When she mentioned that, I immediately thought that is what she was destined to do. She has devoted her entire life to helping others without expecting anything in return.

Come to think of it, that is the very nature of being a teacher. When your students feel like winners, you also feel like a winner. Their successes in life are also your successes.

I love my students so much because I see each and every one of them as my own children. I am able to exude that love in every aspect of my work because I grew up with a mother who was the ultimate embodiment of love. Her dedication to service and her ability to show empathy towards others are attributes that I hold dear to my heart.

My students ask me all the time why I am always smiling and joking around. The reason I why I do that is because I grew up with a mother who always had a smile on her face and joked around, regardless of the adversity she faced throughout her life. She has always had a "glass half-full" outlook on life, which is perhaps the reason why I always believe my students have the ability to be stellar scholars if they approach every challenge with a "glass half-full" mindset. The very attributes that allow me to be an effective teacher in the classroom are the same attributes that make Dorothy A. Mensah the best mother a boy could ever have. My mother's spirit lives within me every day, which is why I can definitively say that I am my mother's child.

$\mathcal{L}$ESSON #1

φ

EVERY TEACHER HAS A "MRS. MARTIN" IN THEM

MY EDUCATIONAL JOURNEY STARTED as a special education student, a label that I would maintain throughout my elementary school years. From first to fourth grade, I attended Laurel Elementary School in Bloomfield, CT. Looking back, I assumed that Laurel was better equipped to provide my special education services than the other elementary schools in the neighborhood. Regardless of what the rationale was, it proved to be the perfect fit for me. That is not to say that I didn't have my share of emotional trauma. Although I appreciated the education I received at Laurel, my time at the school came with many personal challenges. The lingering stigma of being a special education student attributed to my inability to connect socially with other children.

I'm not the first person who has struggled with childhood trauma. As a matter of fact, there is a growing population of special education students in this nation dealing with trauma. According to a recent study by the National Survey on Children's Health, 47% of children in the United States had experienced at least one adverse childhood experience such as a family death, an act of violence, or abuse while nearly 22% had experienced at least two adverse childhood experiences. This growing trend has forced schools nationwide to place more emphasis on social-emotional learning in the classroom.

To ensure that special education students are receiving the social and emotional support they need, more schools have adopted the co-teaching model where the general education teacher and special education teacher are paired in the same classroom. The presence of both teachers assures that appropriate interventions will be in place for students with social-emotional challenges. Given the challenges I experienced in school, the co-teaching approach would have been a great help to me.

The mistreatment I received from the mainstream students made me fully aware of where I stood within the school's social hierarchical order. I felt like a second-class citizen within my own school. Being a second-class citizen meant being considered not cool enough to sit with the popular kids during lunchtime. Being a second-class citizen meant being subjected to a barrage of jokes about my significantly darker skin color and West African heritage. I remember being called such names as "Yoo-Hoo", "Black & Crispy", and "Hershey's Chocolatey" all because I was so much darker in complexion than most of the kids in school.

The Lion King jokes were a huge hit with the crowd and they certainly made it a point to run those jokes to the ground. Being a second-class citizen meant spending a good portion of the school day in a self-contained classroom with other special education students, some of whom were diagnosed with more severe learning disabilities such as autism and Down syndrome. Even though I was placed in the general education class during the time periods for Social Studies and Science, I still wasn't treated as an equal to the other students.

After all those negative experiences, you are probably wondering how I can say Laurel Elementary School was the perfect fit for me. It was because my homeroom teacher, Mrs. Brenda Martin, made it possible for me to overcome my obstacles. Her influence during my first, second, and fourth-grade years played a major part in my teaching career. Since graduating from Laurel 24 years ago, I have not seen or spoken to Mrs. Martin. In recent years, she's been heavy on my mind.

Now that I am a teacher, I want to share with her how much of an impact she's had in my life on a personal and professional level. When times were tough, Mrs. Martin's classroom was a sanctuary. It was the one place where I had the freedom to be my most authentic self. In her classroom, every single person felt like a star. She was lively, vibrant, and always came up with creative ways to make learning fun.

In the three years I was in her class, I honestly can't recall a moment when she yelled at the class. Even on her worst days, she always managed to maintain an even-keeled, mild-mannered demeanor. Nothing fazed her. Regardless of what a child's learning profile was, she always knew what buttons to push in order to get that child to overcome their academic challenges.

I was one of the fortunate students who greatly benefited from her motivational powers. Back then, I was the type of student who got easily frustrated when I didn't understand an assignment or a lesson. In those situations, Mrs. Martin would write me little notes and quietly place them on my desk. The notes always reminded me that I was smart and capable of achieving anything. If a student gave an incorrect response to a question, she would acknowledge the student's thought process that led to the response. By praising our efforts for thinking critically about the question, she gave us the courage to take academic risks and continue to be actively engaged in class.

Mrs. Martin and I were meant to be together. None of the teachers understood me the way she did. Looking back, it took a great deal of patience for her to work with a student who was internally struggling with his confidence and camouflaging his speech issues to shield himself from public ridicule. When I was younger, I did not have the foresight to see how her influence would guide me towards a career in education. The lessons I learned from Mrs. Martin have greatly attributed to my ability to empower my students.

As I stand in front of my own class, I see so much of myself when I look in the eyes of my students. Due to my past experiences, I can empathize with them and build up their confidence in the same way that Mrs. Martin did when I was younger. Every school year, I strive to create a safe classroom environment where every student feels like a star. Over the years, I have employed various strategies to motivate my students. Some of these strategies include homework passes, pizza parties, extra recess, student of the month awards, and positive phone calls to parents. For many of them, the classroom may be the only place in their lives where their presence is valued and validated.

Too many school districts in this country only view students as identification numbers and data points on student achievement data metrics. Not nearly enough attention is being focused on determining how their emotional profiles impact their ability to learn. I was fortunate enough to grow up in an era where developing the whole child was more of a priority than preparing students for standardized testing. As a matter of fact, standardized testing was not as big of a deal back then as it is now.

This was the case for the teachers who grew up in the same era as I did. Back then, schools placed a greater emphasis on teaching the whole child. In other words, the emotional welfare of students was just as much of a priority as their academic abilities. As you will see, the most memorable teachers are the ones who valued the relationships they built with their students.

Nicole Combs, a fifth-grade math and science special education teacher from New Jersey, shares how big of an influence her favorite teacher has been in her personal and professional life:

"My first grade teacher, Ms. Alice Resner, was and is my favorite teacher. I entered her class midway through the school year as my family moved from East New York to Park Slope. So I only had her as a teacher for half the year. Two weeks before second grade, my mom passed away.

In the first week of school, my teacher asked us to write about our summer. As I wrote, I broke down crying. The next thing I remember is Ms. Resner coming to get me. She sat with me in the hall and comforted me until I was ready to go back to class. She checked on me constantly throughout my years in elementary school. She would take me to lunch and always told me how strong I was and how she knows I would go on to do great things.

Twenty-six years later, we still keep in contact. She taught me that being a teacher is more than just making sure students can pass a test. Although I had my family, they were grieving in their own way. No one knew this seven-year-old felt alone, not even Ms. Resner, but just her checking on me made a huge impact. Now, as a teacher, I let my students know that I am here for them."

In Nicole's case, Ms. Resner's response to the trauma she experienced from her mother's passing was the foundation for their life-long relationship. For many educators of color, including myself, we yearn to have that one teacher who looks like us and can relate to us culturally. Many of us don't find that teacher until we reach college. Erin Johnson, a kindergarten teacher at Grover Cleveland Mastery Charter

School in Philadelphia, was fortunate to find that special teacher as a second grader:

"My favorite teacher growing up was my second grade teacher, Mrs. Lindner. She was my only Black teacher from grades K-12. When I was seven, I wasn't able to articulate why she was my favorite teacher. It was not until I became a teacher, standing before a classroom full of little brown faces did I discover what made her so special. Mrs. Lindner looked like me. In a predominantly white school, I found someone who I could relate to. It's imperative that children of color see people who look like them in the classroom, and I want to be the 'Mrs. Lindner' for my students. Mrs. Lindner was firm, but I knew that she loved me. I find myself trying to find that balance that she achieved so effortlessly."

As evidenced by these testimonies, it is clear that our favorite teachers laid the foundation for what it means to be a life changer in the classroom. It is for this reason that we aspire to carry out their legacies and be those life changers for our students. Twenty years from now, our students are not going to remember all the lessons we taught them nor will their future employers ask for their standardized test scores when they interview. Hopefully, what they will remember more than anything else are the different ways in which we took a vested interest in their education and provided valuable lessons that have helped to shape their outlooks on life.

Our hope is that the life lessons we impart to them will help them to navigate the many experiences that life has to offer like parenthood, home ownership, death, and marriage. If our words of wisdom can help shape them into independent thinkers who can critically assess each situation and make informed decisions that will enhance the quality of their lives, then we have done our jobs. That is the mark of a great teacher.

SUMMARY

Take a moment to think about your favorite teacher, a role model, a family member, or any individual you highly admire. Now ask yourself the following questions:

- *Who was your "Mrs. Martin" growing up?*
- *What important life lessons did this individual teach you?*
- *What were the specific qualities that made him/her an important role model in your teaching career?*
- *What type of impact did this individual have on your life?*

Your responses to these questions will more than likely help shape your identity as a teacher. If you are trying to figure out what your teaching style is going to be, look no further than the positive role models who have had a major influence in your life. For some of you, it might be your mother or father. For others, it might be a blood relative or an influential adult in the community.

Everyone has that one role model who inspired them to be great and changed their life. Personally, that role model was Mrs. Martin. She was the first person who provided me with a template of what it looks like to be a great teacher.

It's no surprise that many of her personal qualities have been embedded in my teaching practice. I can still remember the joy I felt whenever I was in her class and I want my students to have the same learning experience I had. As a teacher, you want to channel your "Mrs. Martin" and do everything to emulate the positive impact that he or she had in your life so that your students can be the beneficiaries of your hard work.

IDENTITY TALK
WITH AN EDUCATOR

———

Jami Witherell is a 2nd grade teacher at the Newton School, which is a part of the Greenfield Public School District in Massachusetts. A national recipient of the Grinspoon Award for Excellence in Teaching, Jami has dedicated her teaching career to championing social justice education issues in the classroom. Most importantly, her personal story serves as an inspiration for young people who are struggling with their self-image and various forms of emotional and mental trauma.

In this interview, Jami recounts some of the most traumatic moments in her childhood and pays homage to the educators who have supported her throughout her career.

Q: Why did you want to become a teacher? Was there a particular moment in your life that motivated you to pursue this career path?

A: For a long time, I wanted to be my 5th grade teacher. Then, I wanted to be more than a teacher and dreamed of a career in social justice education. During my freshman year at UMASS Amherst, I sat in Women's Studies 187 with Professor Deschamps, and as she strode toward the stage, it occurred to me that at 18, she was the very first educator of color I ever had. It overwhelmed me. To listen to her lecture was like being at a rock concert. You hung onto every cadence and leaned in like you were hearing something for the very first time. I was inspired and in awe. I went home after her riveting lecture with a confidence that I would not let other children wait until they were 18 for someone who looked like them to stand in the front of the room.

Q: Describe your earliest introduction to teaching. What type of work were you doing? What were your initial impressions?

A: I am a trans-racial adoptee from Chile. My adoptive family is full to the brim with educators. I remember visiting them in their classrooms and I loved watching them teach. I also remember being regaled with stories from the classroom at a young age. My grandfather was a teacher in a one-room schoolhouse where he met my grandmother, so in a way, teachers grew up around me. In terms of teaching in the classroom myself, I was in eighth grade when my social studies teacher sent my best friend and I to several elementary schools to do a presentation on prejudice. It remains one of the best early introductions into teaching. I remember thinking as an eighth grader there are SO many moving parts. You have to get their attention, wait until they are really listening, repeat, repeat, explain, listen, wait, and that it seemed like so much fun, but a lot of work.

Q: Who was your favorite teacher growing up? What important life lessons did this individual teach you? How has this individual influenced your teaching style?
A: The touch points of favorite educators have dotted my entire childhood. My fourth grade teacher, Mr. Moriarty, undid a lot of the damage done by my third grade teacher, who had me scrubbing my skin to be lighter each night just to feel like I was worth something, and cut off all my hair to hide my curls. He was just available, let me be me, and chose to see me when others did not. My fifth grade teacher, Karen Willard, is some 25 years later, my friend and my guardian angel. She wrangled 32 of us with love, sight, and the unending belief that we could be anything and do anything. As our little worlds fell apart through cancer, divorce, and a myriad of hardships, she always told us that we didn't have to fall victim to those issues. I have yet to meet another educator like her. She left teaching at 30 to raise her kids.

My eighth grade social studies teacher was the most innovative teacher I ever had. I vividly remember we made a list of all the problems of the world, grouped them together and then came up with our top two: prejudice and poverty. We spent the fall semester designing projects with our team to solving prejudice and the spring semester designing projects on poverty. I felt empowered, smart, and seen. He nominated me for student of the month in the spring.

I remember standing with the other white students who had been nominated and he unfurled a typewritten essay about why the team had chosen me. The other teachers all apologized for not having something written but talked adoringly about their students. While Mr. Clark read, I remember thinking to myself, "He talked about me and thought about me when I wasn't in his class." He was proud of me. As a child with two moms, I think I had been waiting my whole life for a white teacher to be proud of me.

In high school, my teachers Aimee Monette, Eileen Doherty, and Gerri Monnier all stepped forward to say they saw the leader in me. They cast me in my one and only school play and recognized my abilities as a writer and a teacher. Gerri Monnier and I shared a moment in teaching that will stay with me always. She was the Child Development teacher who supported the preschool at our high school. I had her for two years and taught four-year-olds in both years.

At the end of my senior year, I had done a case study on Anaise, who I believe is now a graduate of UMass Amherst. She came from a struggling family and had little means financially to buy an end of year gift. I had been working all year and had purchased her a horse set since she loved horses. She loved it and gave us the greatest gift of all! She wrote small folded notes to all the teachers' 17 high school students. When you opened them up, her mom had written "BEST AT:" and then Anaise, in her little writing, wrote what she valued about them. Some were best at snack making, reading, being a buddy, and swing pushing.

By the time everyone had opened theirs, all the best ones had been taken. Mrs. Monnier and I sat deflated in our classroom. "I can assure you, Jami," she said, "You won't be disappointed when you open that paper. She may only be 4, but she really sees you." I unfurled the paper to read, "Jami Best At EVERYTHING." I suppose if I had to sum up what each of these teachers taught me, it was the power of being seen, of being valued, and, in many cases, of being loved. I spent my entire childhood desperately trying to be enough, as many adopted kids do, and these were the people who stopped long enough to confirm that I already was.

Q: Any advice you would like to share to help individuals develop their teaching identities?
A: No one ever "told" me, but I have developed a sense that I am not the most important person in the room. I am not the leader and I do not have all the answers. I am a member of the class family. We love each other, we learn together,

and we value each other in our space. We are a family. The minute I let go of a giant teacher's desk, and the idea that I could answer everything – I became a better teacher.

$\mathcal{L}$ESSON #2

φ

CREATE OPPORTUNITIES
WHERE THEY DON'T EXIST

HAVE YOU EVER FOUND yourself in a situation where you had the urge to do more but you felt that your job limited what you could actually do? You have a grand idea for a program, event, or an initiative that could potentially take your school to the next level but your colleagues are so caught up with their own agendas that they don't view your idea as enough of a priority to give it the attention that it deserves. It may also be a case where your school does not have enough money in the budget to fund your program. Whatever the case may be, you have a decision to make. Do you just go with the flow and allow the inactions of your colleagues to discourage you from moving forward with the idea? Or do you take control of the situation and proactively take the steps necessary to bring your idea to life for the benefit of the school community. Hopefully, you will choose to do the latter of the two options.

In any profession, a strong work ethic is an important attribute to possess but it does not always translate to a climb up in the professional ladder. Performing the specific tasks within your job description at a consistently high level is what you are expected to do. It should be enough to guarantee you a job promotion or an increased level of responsibility with added incentives but, unfortunately, it does not always work out that way. The ability to make a positive impact within your school will require you to proactively seek opportunities that align with the school's vision.

In this specific context, being proactive does not mean taking on every opportunity that comes your way. It simply means taking a need assessment of the school to carve out a role that will showcase your strengths and bring about progressive change. The needs assessment can be done with a student survey or through interviews with multiple staff members. The purpose of the assessment is to gather data and identify any trends that reveal areas where the school can grow.

With any idea that you bring to your principal's attention, the key is to be able to articulate how your idea will address a specific need of the school. It is also imperative to come prepared with a written plan that spells out how your idea will be executed and the various supports you will need to move it forward. A principal will be more inclined to grant their approval when they see that you have taken the time to work out the logistics such as a proposed budget, anticipated class schedule changes, and a timeline detailing the different tasks that need to be completed. Evidence of proactive planning and preparation are the most important components of any idea proposal. The more prepared you are, the better your chances are of moving forward with your idea.

In the early stages of my career, I sometimes found myself wondering why some of my colleagues still had a job when they were constantly doing things that were counterproductive to the social and emotional growth of their students. I even wondered why they were earning more money than me but working half as hard as I was. As I have gained more experience in this profession, I have come to realize that there are certain things that are beyond my control such as the hiring process of staff members or the annual salaries that they earn. Those factors should not distract you from your primary goal, which is to do everything in your power to be a beacon of hope and support for your students. Regardless of what transpires outside of your classroom, your goal is all the motivation you need to push yourself to new heights professionally.

Over the past four years, I have been teaching 7th & 8th grade mathematics at the Joseph Lee School in Boston. Being one of only three Black male lead teachers in the building, I find there are many important contributions I can make to the 80% Black and Latino student body besides just teaching mathematics. I take it as a personal responsibility to support my students. I have to be a change agent and create opportunities for my students so that they are in a position to be successful, even if certain staff members around me do not subscribe to that mindset. That is the very definition of being a leader and advocate for the students.

To stay true to my mission, I have made it a point to create and coordinate incentive programs that will support the academic and behavioral growth of the middle school students. In the time I have worked at the school, very few events and incentives have been organized for the middle school students and that has left a void in their school morale. These students are expected to adhere to school-wide norms and protocols on a daily basis. So much is asked of them but they receive little in return when they meet those expectations. For certain students, they will continue to follow expectations because they are intrinsically motivated but for others, the lack of appreciation from staff members will cause them to develop feelings of apathy towards school. These feelings may be manifested in the form of excessive absenteeism, increased levels of off-task classroom behaviors, or inconsistent effort on classwork and homework assignments.

With that in mind, I saw an opportunity to organize a Sadie Hawkins Dance to increase student attendance and minimize unproductive behaviors within the middle school program. I collaborated with my good friend Al "Ski" McClain to put together the event. Al is a popular and respected community figure here in Boston. Al, a former NBA player, has dedicated the past thirty years of his life organizing youth basketball programs and tournaments as a vehicle to mentor kids in the Dorchester and Roxbury areas of Boston. As a result of this, many kids have proceeded to earn college degrees and mature into productive citizens in their communities.

More importantly, Al already had close relationships with many of the middle school students as a result of their participation in his basketball programs over the years, so I knew that it was something that we could leverage to our advantage when advertising the event. While Al focused on promoting the dance to community members outside of the school, I was responsible for organizing the staff members and promoting the event to the students.

A fashion shop was set up in the principal's office so that students could pick out a full outfit for the dance. Many of the clothes in the shop were donations by staff members and personal purchases I made from the local thrift stores. Although the shop was open to all students, priority was given to students who came from families that couldn't afford a suit, tie, or a formal dress. The shop was open for three weeks and during that time, multiple staff members voluntarily sacrificed their break periods to help out. It was refreshing to see the staff engaging with the students and helping them try on different outfits.

Since this was an incentive dance, students had to earn an invitation in order to attend. To earn an invitation, students had to achieve a 90% attendance rate, adhere to the school's Code of Conduct policy, and demonstrate consistent academic effort in all core content areas within the one-month tracking period. With the dance just around the corner, more staff members volunteered to be involved with the preparation process. As I had envisioned, this dance was shaping up to be a community building affair. From the deejaying to the decorating of the party venue, every aspect of the preparation process was covered by a staff member.

The Sadie Hawkins Dance was a huge success! The middle school students and staff members came to the dance, looking fabulous and dressed to the nines! The dance was packed with all of the essentials: a photo booth, a Best Dressed Contest for students and staff members to flaunt their fashionable outfits down the red carpet, delicious food, live music, and lots of raffle prizes. To be honest, this dance turned out to be much bigger than even I expected and that would not have been possible without the sacrifices, support, and efforts of so many staff members in the Joseph Lee School community.

The students had a rare opportunity to witness the human side of the teachers, and more importantly, their dedication to providing them with a memorable school experience. When I first arrived at the school four years earlier, an event of this magnitude would have been an afterthought because of the negative reputation of the middle school students. The success of the Sadie Hawkins Dance served as a major step in transforming the reputation of the middle school program and, more importantly, it opened the door for me to create more fun incentive events for the students. The potential for more incentive events resulted in middle school students attending school at a higher rate.

All of this success happened because the vision for creating a more positive school atmosphere for the middle school students came to life. When I first thought of the idea for the dance, there were some staff members who were totally against it. I could have allowed their dismissive responses to discourage me from moving forward but I knew, in my heart, that this event had the potential to bridge the school community together to brainstorm solutions for improving the relationship between middle school students and staff members.

SUMMARY

As you work on generating opportunities to enhance your school community and draw on your talents, consider the following points:

1. Be selective with the opportunities you receive

The willingness to be proactive and consistently respond to the call of duty is an important trait to possess in any profession. Sometimes, advancing your career requires you to go above and beyond your job description. This involves creating opportunities that don't exist or simply doing the dirty work that no one else wants to do. The smallest of tasks can potentially lead to bigger and better opportunities. However, you must be mindful of each opportunity that is presented to you because not every opportunity will guarantee you a chance to advance your career. Use your discretion when determining whether a task or opportunity best aligns with your vision for success.

2. Identify the need

Within a school, there are so many needs that certain ones never get addressed. Determine the areas of growth where your school can improve. There isn't a single school that is free from flaws. Similar to human beings, every school has room to grow. Do not overburden yourself by addressing every single need. Focus on the one need where you feel you can make the greatest impact.

3. Develop a plan of action

With any idea or program that you have in mind, you will need to get approval from your principal or school leader. Regardless of whether your school leader possesses a 'hands-off' leadership style or leans more to the 'micromanagement' end of the spectrum, it is imperative that you articulate how they can best support you in your endeavor. They may direct you to resources that can facilitate the preparation process. That being said; be sure to outline the following components when creating your plan:

- The **intended goal of your idea/program**, which should include a brief overview of how it adds value to the school community.
- A **detailed timeline of tasks** that need to be completed to ensure the completion of the goal.

- The **number of staff members** needed to support your idea/program.
- A **proposed budget** with a list of items/resources needed to be purchased.
- Other **logistics** such as scheduling changes, substitute coverage, alternative dates in the event of inclement weather, etc.

The more detailed you are, the greater your chances are of having your idea approved by your principal.

4. Replace passivity with proactivity

Being proactive is all about having a vision for your career and acting on your hunger for greatness. If you keep waiting for opportunities to come to you, you will cheat yourself out of a chance to create the narrative that you want people to know about you. Do not elude what could be the prelude to the opportunity of a lifetime.

IDENTITY TALK
WITH AN EDUCATOR

———

Erica Jones is a perfect example of an educator who proactively followed her heart and created an opportunity that positively impacted the personal welfare of her students and the school, as a whole. During her nine-year career, Erica served as a teacher and a Principal fellow at different schools within the School District of Philadelphia. During her interview, she shares a powerful story about how she identified a specific need at one of her former schools and developed an opportunity for students to serve as leaders within their school community in the midst of major disapproval.

Q: Why did you want to become a teacher? Was there a particular moment in your life that motivated you to pursue this career path?

A: I became an educator because I truly feel that education is the key to unlock limitless potential. Through proper education, one can truly manifest their heart's desires. This idea was instilled in me by my parents at a very young age. In spite of me being born into a family where no one had graduated from college, many fell victim to the prison system and very few took the opportunity to travel outside of Brooklyn, I knew that I could make the life I wanted if I just made it to college and educated myself. Truly believing this at a young age put me on a different trajectory than those of my peers. Once I attained my Master's degree in Education, it was my mission to return to a neighborhood similar to one I grew up in to influence the minds of our youth, so that they too could manifest whatever it was that their heart desired.

Q: Describe a moment in your teaching career when you felt the urge to do more than what was stated in your job description but experienced major opposition from your colleagues. What was your response to the opposition?

A: This particular experience caused me many sleepless nights because I could not believe how the implicit bias nature of teachers truly affect the potential they see within their students. Being a proud Black woman, I took offense at the position one of my former grade partners took when our students had the opportunity to create real change in their community.

I established a partnership between one of my former schools and a local non-profit organization that worked to empower students to become agents of change within their community while learning about their civil liberties. I worked with this organization in the past and saw my students achieve greatness. In a previous year, my students started an anti-gun violence campaign where they petitioned community members and got the attention from Pennsylvania Senator Bob Casey as well as a written letter from President Obama in recognition of their work in the community. I was very proud of the work my students put in to raise awareness as well as the position the organization played in educating and assisting them.

The following year is where my newly assigned grade partner was introduced to the work I was doing with my students and the organization. In the beginning phase, she seemed to be extremely supportive of the students choosing to work on beautifying their concrete jungle of a schoolyard, where students were hurt often due to scraped knees on uneven pavement. Not to mention, there was no playground or play equipment. Students were often bored in the schoolyard which often resulted in fights. My colleague assisted our students in surveying the student body and lunchtime brainstorming sessions which were all a part of their action plan.

Once she was told that City Council President, Darrell Clarke, wanted to come to hear about the children's concern; that was when this woman completely flipped the entire script. Now all of a sudden this was a "dog and pony show", and "No way were these children ever going to get City Council to do anything". Then she went on to attack my character and integrity.

To make matters worse, she left the children and myself hanging on the day of their presentation to Council President Clarke. Mind you, their presentation was held literally down the hall in my classroom. I decided that I would continue to support the students without her assistance at that point. By the end of the year, my students were able to get money earmarked specifically for the beautification of the Tanner Duckrey schoolyard as well as some upgrades (seating area and a garden area).

Many people in education tend to use the clichéd line "children first". However, many do not realize that whatever they believe subconsciously, about the children they serve, will inherently rear its head regardless of how ugly or beautiful it may be. Dig deep down inside to find and know the truth about the children whom you serve. As with me, during those times of adversity, it will be those inherent truths that lead you towards action while educating our youth.

Q: Any advice you would like to share to help individuals develop their teaching identities?
A: Know yourself and be that person authentically!! Continue to grow and educate yourself. Identify the

miserable naysayers and toxic people in your work environment and stay away! Take a personal interest in each child that comes before you. The words and actions you display even for a moment may truly stick with that child for a lifetime. Most importantly, always remember to exercise self-care! A toxic teacher tends to create a toxic classroom. Be that teacher who inspires children to live out their limitless dreams.

$\mathcal{L}$ESSON #3

φ

MONEY CAN'T
BUY YOU LOVE

IF YOU ASK THE average teacher what motivated them to embark on a career in teaching, I'm pretty sure they'd say it was a love for children, rather than making money. There is no sum of money that will cause your love to increase or decrease because the love for the work is unwavering. For many teachers throughout the nation, the act of teaching is emotionally tasking because today's children enter the classrooms with needs that transcend the academic realm.

In a recent Time article, many public school teachers expressed the need to remain in their underpaid positions because of their moral obligation to their students. They are afraid of leaving their students to fend for themselves within an education system set up for them to fail. These teachers are cognizant of the inequities that exist within the education system and want to ensure their students that they are equipped with the tools necessary to survive in the society.

According to Brianne Solomon, an art teacher from West Virginia, she feels like she has to be a "surrogate parent or sibling to her more than 180 students" she serves each day. She further adds, "So many of our students come from broken homes, and you have to pick up the slack. You have to combat all of that. These kids don't come to school to learn. They come to be loved." An emotional connection like the one that Brianne had with her students is one of the primary reasons why teachers stay in the teaching profession.

The dedication and passion that teachers have for this work go beyond the classroom. In many states, there are teachers who are sacrificing personal time with their families to fulfill their job obligations. Due to increases in classroom sizes, teachers have found it difficult to complete all their work at school. This has resulted in them bringing home papers to grade "late into the evenings, for hours on weekends, and throughout their school-sanctioned breaks." Since teachers earn fixed annual salaries, they do not earn overtime pay for the extra work they do.

In fact, Walt DelGirono, a retired special education teacher in Delaware, decided one year to keep a running log of the total hours he worked outside of school. This included after-school time during the work week in addition to weekend hours, holidays, and summer vacation. Based on his records, he accumulated a total of about 2,000 hours, which is the equivalent of 40 hours per week over a 50-week period. These numbers are comparable to the amount of time that non-educators work in other professions.

For individuals who are starting out in entry-level positions like a paraprofessional or a teaching assistant, money can be an issue. Entry level employees are typically signed to a ten-month contract which means you need a summer job in order to continue earning an income until the start of the next school year. I did not love working during the summer but it was an opportunity for me to not only earn income but continue to acquire valuable teaching experience.

As a developing educator, summer teaching jobs present a golden opportunity for you to sharpen your instructional practices. Typically, veteran teachers do not pursue summer teaching positions because they elect to recuperate their bodies after teaching for an entire school year. As a result, there are multiple vacancies for teaching assistants and other non-certified teaching professionals looking to work on their craft. Even if you are not teaching, working as a summer camp counselor is the next best thing because you can still test out behavioral management strategies on the children.

Before earning my initial teaching license, I worked at three different schools in a support staff or teaching assistant role. In each stop, times were difficult financially but the potential for career growth and networking with more experienced educators motivated me to keep working. Of the three schools, the most rewarding and, by far, the most financially challenging experience was working as a school-based corps member for EducationWorks at the Tanner Duckrey School. The opportunity to be exposed to the inner workings of a public school and to be surrounded by established teachers more than compensated for the little money that I was earning.

LIFE AT EDUCATION WORKS

EducationWorks was my first employer after graduating from Temple University. Since it was a non-profit governmental organization, the pay was not great, as non-profits are often not very well funded. I witnessed a lot of my college friends earn job offers from major corporate companies. Many of them were either architecture majors or engineering majors so as soon as they graduated, they had a job guaranteed for them. Immediately, they started with annual salaries in the range of $60,000 to $80,000. When you're a broke 20 to 21-year-old college graduate and spent your undergraduate years surviving off of work-study jobs, an annual salary within a range of $60,000 to $80,000 feels like a million dollars!

Upon completion of my AmeriCorps term, I would earn a lump sum education award for continuing my education. In order to get the education award, you had to complete two consecutive terms with AmeriCorps and, upon completion of those terms, you earned an award worth $4,725. I was earning a government stipend of about $215 every two weeks, which meant that I was only earning about $5,160 per year. The monthly rent for the apartment I was staying at the time was $750. I was sharing the apartment with two college friends, which meant I was only responsible for contributing $250 monthly towards the rent payments.

With the addition of utility costs, my monthly contribution rose anywhere between $325 to $350, depending on the amount of electricity and water we used throughout the month. Without the help of my college friends, it would have been impossible for me to independently survive off of my government stipends. I was working a minimum of 40 hours every week just to earn peanuts for all the hard work I was putting in. To put my living situation in perspective, I was left with a remaining amount of $80 to $105 for food and necessities, which left me with only $10 to $35 of disposable income.

For two years, I lived a minimalist life using a sleeping bag and public transportation. Hard financial times forced me to become an introverted individual. After paying off my monthly expenses, I barely had money to engage in fun activities like going to the movie theater, visiting the bowling alley, or attending a live sporting event. Furthermore, much of my time was fully devoted to working at the summer camp and just trying to get through the upcoming school year at Tanner Duckrey School.

During the school year, I was working 9 to 10 hours daily, which translated to 45 to 50 hours weekly. For the first 6 hours of the workday, I, along with my team members, provided classroom assistance to teachers and monitored the students during non-instructional periods such as lunch and recess. The remainder of the workday was spent working the after-school program, which ran from 3:00 pm to 6:00 pm. As physically and mentally exhausting as it was, we embraced the workday grind because we knew that our efforts were having a positive impact on the students at Duckrey.

It was easy for me to report to work everyday because I was a part of a team that was professional, supportive, and shared a passion for providing students with the most positive school experience on a daily basis. All of us were very proactive by nature and always strived to go beyond the call of duty. We all weren't getting paid a whole lot of money for the collective work we were doing but it didn't matter to us. Working for EducationWorks was a labor of love for all of us and we all approached the job with a love and passion that touched the hearts of the many students we serviced.

SHAPING THE TEACHER IDENTITY

SUMMARY

It is no secret that teaching is far from being the most lucrative profession. When searching for teaching opportunities, don't place too much of an emphasis on how much the job pays. Unless you possess a Master's degree or a teaching license, don't expect to find any high-paying teaching positions. Since your main intention is to get your foot in the door, you should consider working for a school that provides you with the greatest potential for career growth. Knowledge and tutelage from seasoned educators are a premium! The most lucrative job offers don't always guarantee you the greatest potential to grow as a teacher. Stephanie Noriega, a second-grade teacher from Newark, NJ, grasped at the opportunity to gain leadership experience by accepting an interim role as her school's after-school program coordinator, in spite of the fact that she would not receive extra pay:

> *"Just recently, I was asked to cover the Aftercare*
> *Coordinator position while the original coordinator*
> *would be gone on maternity leave. As a current graduate*
> *school student for Educational Leadership, I thought this*

was a perfect opportunity to be in charge of an organization. This would mean having to balance my original duties as well as solve issues such as aftercare club coverage. As soon as some of my colleagues heard the news, they immediately asked if I requested more money. I replied, "no" and they advised me that I should have asked about this before agreeing. I explained that I was honored that they trusted me with such responsibility and that I was thankful for the experience. To me, it's not always about getting more money, but to learn from the overall leadership opportunity in general."

Furthermore, money does not always equate to happiness. I have witnessed many colleagues return back to the classroom after many years working in leadership and administration because they missed having the daily interaction with students, as well as the ability to directly teach students on a daily basis. Even though moving back to the classroom resulted in a pay cut, they had no regrets about their decision because they regained their joy and passion for teaching. Even though money is a necessity to support your family, it should not always be the main factor that dictates the direction you take in your career.

IDENTITY TALK
WITH AN EDUCATOR

————

Bernadette Thornton-Giles currently serves as a Teacher Peer-Assistant for Boston Public Schools, where her main role is to provide coaching, support, and mentorship to teachers throughout the district in an effort to strengthen student learning and teacher performance. A twenty-year veteran in Boston Public Schools, Bernadette has an extensive history of mentoring teachers to engage in culturally responsive teaching practices that will lead to student success. In this interview, Bernadette discusses her earliest introduction to teaching and how she has maintained her passion for teaching in a time where many educators nationwide are leaving the profession to pursue more lucrative job opportunities.

Q: Describe your earliest introduction to teaching. What type of work were you doing? What were your initial impressions?

A: My earliest introduction to teaching came when I was a social worker for the Department of Social Services in Boston. The majority of children on my caseload were in the care and custody of the department, which meant I, as their worker, attended all their IEP meetings and any other school meetings that the foster parent or group home were unwilling to attend. I began to realize that I could do more for children in the classroom as opposed to meeting them under less than ideal circumstances as their social worker.

My initial impression was that I would be given all that I needed in order to meet the students' needs as their teacher. I quickly found out that, like social work, the odds are continuously stacked against me and my students, as the basics are often not enough. My first year of teaching was in Cambridge, MA. I taught fifth grade to a largely white population of students who were very privileged. I knew that I was supposed to be serving the population of students that looked like me and had similar experiences to my own, so the following year I took a second grade position at a Boston school. There is where I learned that all things were not created equal and many adults didn't expect much from the students they were working with.

Q: What was your starting annual salary in your first year of teaching? Knowing that teachers, in general, are severely underpaid nationwide, what has specifically motivated you to keep working in the field of education for so many years?

A: When I came into teaching, it was a career change. I got a Master's degree in Education. Therefore, I was paid a little more than the average first-year teacher. My annual salary was about $35,000. The work that we do is a calling more so than a career. I fully understand how important my presence and your presence are to our students. I have direct proof within my own children of what can happen when you have a dedicated and skilled educator working with your child. I also have experienced the antithesis of this as well. What we do improves the life trajectory for young people. That's not a career...that's a calling.

Q: Has there ever been a time when you have considered leaving the field of education to accept a more lucrative job offer but declined it to remain in the classroom?

A: This is a great question because I believe both young teachers and veteran teachers alike have had these thoughts. Many times, it is due to the mounting changes and requirements that are placed on teachers, without providing them with support and resources. The answer is yes, but I never have, because I don't know of any other job that would stretch me, frustrate me, motivate me, inspire me, mobilize me, and fulfill me like being an educator does.

Q: In your opinion, do you believe that the issue of teacher's pay will discourage people from considering a career in education moving forward?

A: Yes, I do. This is also seen within our racially diverse populations as well. Many non-whites are being encouraged to go to college and seek out more lucrative paying jobs. I don't believe it is because there is a negative attitude towards teaching. Quite simply put, you are able to do more for the village when you are bringing in the big bucks. That alone speaks to the level of influence you can have over what happens in your community. I strongly believe in "grassroots efforts," but many of our people struggle and don't want to see their children do the same, therefore they are conveying a different message to them.

Q: Any advice you would like to share to help individuals develop their teaching identities?

A: This is going to sound cliché but be true to who you are. This means that a reflective practice is paramount. Reflect on where you are in your own personal journey and don't let the revelations scare you. Many times, we find out that we are just as insecure and flawed in areas that we may need to ask for help in. Build a network of trustworthy and knowledgeable people that can help with those areas. I like to say you should always have at least one dreamer in your corner. The dreamer is going to constantly motivate you when you are at your lowest and feeling like you have hit a wall in your progress. Sometimes you will be the dreamer for someone else in the teaching profession as well.

$\mathcal{L}$ESSON #4

φ

ADVERSITY BIRTHS OPPORTUNITIES FOR PERSONAL GROWTH

THE CHALLENGES AND OBSTACLES of my early education and career were so challenging that I questioned whether I had what it takes to be a teacher. I could devote an entire book to sharing with you all of the adverse situations I have faced as an educator but that is not my intention. However, I would like to share a personal story that best illustrates how adversity has impacted my career as a teacher.

BAPTISM BY FIRE

It was around November 2007 when I was called into the principal's office at West Philadelphia Achievement Charter School (WPACES), a small K-5 school located in West Philadelphia, to discuss a new job assignment. Initially, the school hired me to serve as the Instructional Assistant for the fifth grade classrooms but due to the increasing amount of teacher turnover, I was asked by the school's leadership team to serve as the substitute teacher for a fourth-grade class that had already lost four teachers within the first few months of the school year. They needed me to hold down the fort for a month while they searched for a long-term replacement.

As you can imagine, the fourth-grade classroom was a space marred by chaos and dysfunction. It was everything that you would expect from a classroom that had gone through four different teachers and was lacking in structure. I wondered how I was going to pull off the feat of establishing a culture of order and structure in a classroom where the students had witnessed a revolving door of teachers entering and leaving. When I met the students, it was obvious that they were yearning for structure and normalcy within their classroom.

They were eager to learn but their way of manifesting that desire was by exhibiting attention-seeking behaviors that often got them into a world of trouble. How exactly is a student supposed to react when they experience a new teacher every single month? This was going to be a difficult task but I was ready to give it my best effort. I was not provided any lesson plans or given a sense of what the class had been learning up to that point. All I was told by the principals was that I needed to keep the seat warm for the long-term replacement.

Once again, I was thrown into another situation where I had to figure things out on my own. As I scanned the classroom, I tried to look for any materials or resources I could salvage in order to teach the students. Luckily, I came across a bunch of math textbooks and a library consisting of leveled reading books, which was great because I could focus my attention on teaching the two most important content areas: math and reading. Another thing I recognized was that there was no academic schedule posted anywhere in the classroom so I went ahead and created a new schedule from scratch. Once I had the materials organized, I just jumped right in and started providing instruction to the students. Naturally, the first official day was spent doing introductions and orienting students to class norms and routines.

Thankfully, the principals assigned an additional staff member to assist me in the classroom. She was a retired teacher who was hired to serve as a teaching assistant for the younger grades. Together, we started to turn things around in the classroom. At the time, I did not have a clue about the specific math and reading skills that fourth graders were supposed to learn so I ended up improvising my lessons.

For math, I chose to spend much of the time helping students strengthen their basic foundation skills. This involved helping them learn basic multiplication and division facts. For reading, I divided the students into six color-coded groups. Each group represented a particular reading level. Using the leveled books in the classroom library, I was able to conduct guided reading lessons with each of the groups. Since many of the students were reading well below grade level, the lessons primarily focused on reading fluency, word decoding strategies, and comprehension. Now that real learning was finally happening in the classroom, I could shift my focus to decorating the classroom.

With the entire teacher turnover that took place, it was no surprise that the classroom was not decorated. None of the previous four teachers stayed in the classroom long enough to really get settled in. I was happy to see the students finally getting learning done but I knew there was still something missing. The classroom was in dire need of a makeover. It needed to be transformed into a space that was aesthetically pleasing to the eye. Students needed to be energized when they walk into the classroom. Where would this source of energy come from?

To answer that question, I reflected on my grade school experience and thought about the various components that made the classroom a welcoming place to learn. I remember seeing inspirational quotes and colorful posters plastered all over the walls. My teachers also had bulletin boards designated for displaying graded tests of students who scored an 80% or above. The tests were tattered with cool stickers and written superlative comments ranging from "You're a Superstar!" to "Great Job!!"

As great as most of my teachers were, I would be remiss if I did not acknowledge the impact that a well-decorated classroom had on my learning. The different components brought about an energy that permeated the entire classroom and empowered me to be the best scholar I could be. The classroom possessed an aesthetic quality that injected life into my spirit. The classroom was my home away from home. I felt safe, secure, welcomed, and valued every time I walked through the door. More than anything, I wanted this fourth-grade classroom to embody those feelings I had when I was in grade school. If they came into a clean classroom that was neat and organized, it would promote a culture of excellence. That was the ultimate goal in mind.

To bring this vision to life, I stayed after school to embellish the barren classroom walls. This would end up being a one-week process that required the logging of consecutive 10 to 12-hour work days. The after-school time was also spent on lesson planning and organizing materials. During that week, I was arriving at school at about 6:30 am and, on most days, I wouldn't leave until around 5:00 pm. The extra hours after school did not translate to a pay increase. Nevertheless, transforming that classroom gave me a sense of satisfaction and accomplishment that could not be equated with any sum of money. The ultimate gift was seeing the eyes of those fourth-grade students widen in amazement as they took in the full view of their newly embellished classroom. For the first time in a very long time, their home away from home actually felt like home.

All of this transformative work did not stop in the classroom. It would be evident in the orderly manner that the class transitioned in the hallways and the way they behaved in their elective classes like Art, Science, and Music. At the end of the day, the students appreciated the time and effort I put into creating a structured environment that they had not experienced for much of the school year.

Even though our time was short-lived, we really grew together as a unit. The students reinvigorated their interest in learning and, in turn, pushed me to take my teaching skills to another level. Granted, I still felt that I could have done a better job as far as providing them with more rigorous instruction but I knew that was not my main reason for being there. My main goal was to rebuild the classroom culture and provide some short-term stability to a class that had been yearning for it for so long. This would set the foundation for the long-term substitute teacher who would end up relieving me of my duties and taking over for the remainder of the school year.

SUMMARY

One of the most important lessons I have learned about this profession is that adversity always provides you with an opportunity to build mental strength and character. The manner in which you respond to adversity will determine whether you stay in the profession for 20 days or remain in it for 20 years. Given the overwhelming amount of responsibility that is placed on the teacher's shoulders, it is inevitable that you will encounter your share of adverse situations.

My advice to you is to fully embrace the challenges that come in your path and view each one as a learning opportunity. Even the most accomplished teachers dealt with their share of adversity before evolving into the educators they are today. Chanelle Peters, a kindergarten teacher from Washington D.C., is no stranger to adversity. Her story is a perfect example of how new educators enter the field with a romanticized view of teaching only to be hit with a healthy dose of reality:

"I was fresh out of graduate school, after earning my Master's in Early Childhood Education. I was a career

changer, so I was embarking on my first Lead Teacher position. I joined the faculty of a public charter school in Washington D.C. with an optimistic spirit believing that I was going to make a difference in children's lives.

Unfortunately, in a short two months, I found myself seated in an administrator's office, as I was told that "this wasn't a good fit" and I would "find my niche" elsewhere. Unrealistic administrative expectations and environmental factors, beyond my control, resulted in my being forced to leave my first teaching position. It took almost an entire year for me to regain confidence not only in myself as an educator, but also in my decision to pursue education as my profession. This experience taught me that teachers need administrators who support them, mentor them, and respect them."

As you gain experience in this profession, you start to realize that every day is a learning opportunity. When challenges arise, you need to be prepared to rise above them and extract the essential lessons. Stephanie Noriega has adopted this "glass half-full" philosophy and managed to maintain a positive attitude in spite of the high teacher turnover rates at her charter school:

"At the charter school that I teach at, each classroom is supposed to have a teacher and an instructional assistant.

Unfortunately, due to unforeseen circumstances such as teacher turnover or new teacher assignments, I have been working alone in my classroom. Although I find it extremely difficult having to work alone and not having the additional support in the classroom like everyone else, I am realizing that this experience is only making me stronger. I realize I am in competition with myself each and every day. Am I able to check homework faster than yesterday and at the same time be efficient?

Thankfully, I have a group of students who understand that I am alone and show great support in the class. The students who complete their assignments quickly are able to help me around the class or even help a partner out. I feel like although we are short by one adult, students seem to fill in the void. Regardless, I am grateful for another learning experience as I also learn about being more patient, time management, and effectiveness."

Adversity is a natural part of a teacher's progression. There is no such thing as a perfect teacher. You have teachers who have been in the profession for 20 years and acknowledge that there are certain aspects of their craft they are still trying to master. As teachers, we always tell our students to have a growth mindset when it comes to their ability to master specific skills. That same concept needs to be applied to teachers. The best teachers achieve longevity in this profession because of their resilient approach to adversity and their commitment to improving their craft. Here are four tips that can help you instill a growth mindset in yourself:

1. Focus on the difficult tasks

It is human nature to become complacent once you settle into a comfortable teaching rhythm. This notion is especially true for veteran teachers. You find yourself teaching the same lessons without making any adjustments or employing the same teaching strategies year after year. In the back of your mind, you realize what you're doing is not producing the desired learning outcomes, but you continue to do it because it is convenient and prevents you from doing extra work. Complacency is a hindrance to your growth because it causes you to develop a false reality about your value as an educator.

This false reality camouflages your deepest insecurities and inhibits you from addressing your challenges. Rather than focus on what you identify as areas of strength, work on the areas of your practice where you are not as strong. For instance, I have one colleague, an English teacher, who has a phobia for computers because she struggles with typing and operating the Microsoft Office applications. In the past, she didn't assign her students learning tasks on the computer because she didn't want to go through the process of learning how to use the applications.

One summer, she finally overcame her fear by enrolling in a professional development course on educational technology tools. Through this course, she learned how to use Google Classroom, which she now uses exclusively for essay assignments and other writing tasks. Most importantly, her students are benefiting from a more engaging learning experience. In order to maximize the potential of our scholars, you have to be prepared to address your challenge areas so that you can be a more complete teacher.

2. Be a solution-oriented teacher

As you reflect on your teaching practices, brainstorm different ways in which you can improve. Be open to researching educational articles and books that will help to develop your ideas around such aspects as teaching pedagogy, learning task differentiation, and classroom management. Over the course of a long school year, you will experience many failed ideas and find yourself having to start over. If your idea flops the first time, do not get discouraged. Sometimes, all it takes is a slight tweak to an assignment or a full revamping of a lesson in order to achieve student growth. Teachers who possess a growth mindset are always working to resolve any challenges that arise in their classrooms.

3. Seek constructive feedback

How can you become a better teacher if you don't receive constructive feedback about your performance? You don't have to wait until you receive your formal evaluation from an administrator before taking steps to improve your performance. Proactively seek out a colleague who you trust and have them visit your classroom to observe you teach. It doesn't hurt to have another set of eyes in the classroom so they can provide further analysis on your performance.

4. Reflect, reflect, reflect

At the end of each school day, take some time to reflect on your performance. How did your students respond to your instruction? Are there certain parts of your lesson that need to be tweaked or does the entire lesson need to be revamped? Which students need extra support with the new skills you taught? These are some of the questions that you want to ask yourself as you reflect. This is an important practice to adopt because it keeps you grounded mentally and reiterates the idea that you are a work-in-progress.

IDENTITY TALK
WITH AN EDUCATOR

———

Erica Mason is an educational communications specialist who has international and domestic experience in training, curricula development, and teacher education. A former Boston Public Schools teacher, Erica has spent the past two decades educating children and serving in teacher leadership positions in various countries throughout the world, including Zambia, Democratic Republic of Congo, the United Kingdom, Myanmar, and South Korea.

Erica shares her early beginnings as a teacher and opens up about how, as a foreigner, she has navigated the many challenges she has experienced in building trusted relationships with school administrators and parents in the different countries she has served.

Q: Why did you want to become a teacher? Was there a particular moment in your life that motivated you to pursue this career path?

A: I had a definitive moment when I chose to be a teacher. I was a sophomore in high school and in a terrible English class. The teacher was strict and incredibly intelligent, but she was unforgiving and it was difficult to connect with her. She taught grammar and American literature, and her choices were old and bland (Winesburg, Ohio, The Scarlet Letter, The Romantic Poets, Hemingway - almost all white, old, and orthodox, with the exception of Toni Morrison). She had dyed red hair. Almost all of my friends knew what they wanted to do as a career, and I felt a bit lost, and under pressure to choose something.

As my mind wandered in her class, I thought, "I can do this. I can teach." It was a really affirmative moment, and I felt really confident. I was a leader among my peers, I always talked too much, I connected with kids. I explored the idea further to think about which subject I would teach. I didn't want to teach English because that class was terrible, so I chose something I did like: history. Ironically, non-stop, I used that that horrid English teacher's etymology lessons in my own teaching career.

Looking back, I really feel like teaching was an intuitive, obvious choice. I like communicating with others and I am genuinely interested in the ideas of young people of all ages. I understand their logic, which is totally different from that of adults. I like the autonomy of teaching, the fact that I'm not sitting at a desk all day, and that each day is different from the next. And, for me, teaching is so much more than a classroom job. It's a role in society that signals someone who hears and uses what they hear to enrich the lives of others, either by guiding them or connecting them (to others, resources, themselves).

Q: Describe a moment in your teaching career when you faced a major challenge. What specific lesson did you learn from that challenge and how did it help support your growth as an educator?

A: In my first year of teaching, I faced some of my toughest challenges. I was inexperienced and immature, and my background did not prepare me for many of the challenges I was going to face. The school demographic enrollment had changed dramatically as the result of gentrification, and I had a class of kindergarten students that came from different economic, ethnic, and religious backgrounds to the rest of the school, where the majority of the students were free-lunch. Twenty-two out of my twenty-six students were white, one was Black and three were Asian, all three adopted. Only two had single moms; three had LGBTQ parents, and none were immigrants.

The majority of students in my class were the first child in their family in school, which meant their parents were heavily involved, even more so because the parents had jobs (or the freedom not to work) and local homes that allowed them to visit and participate more. The school was very small- one class per grade, and one special education class per grade (very little inclusion). My class had nothing in common with the rest of the school. I was also trained as a secondary education teacher and had no idea how to manage kindergarteners. This year was a steep learning curve for me – how to prepare in general, create curriculum, deal with parents, deal with administration, manage a classroom, connect students to other cultures and backgrounds, understand context and learning styles, and support students who needed help.

The lesson I consistently cite from that time when I trained other teachers was among one of the most important of my career. When I was training as a teacher, our professor told us to simplify each lesson as much as possible, get it down to the basics in order to teach it well. That year, I watched another kindergarten teacher tell the students they were going to cut a piece of paper in half. I thought to myself that the first, most-simple step was to fold the paper in half, corner to corner. But I watched the teacher hold up a pair of scissors and ask the students to do the same. She stuck her thumb through the round hole, two fingers through the long one, and levered her fingers back and forth. The first step, of course, was not about cutting the paper at all. It was learning how to use the scissors.

This lesson is a real metaphor for teaching, not just a lesson on how to teach. There have been many times as a teacher of older students where I have had to knock down what has been built, go back, and re-teach the 'scissors moment' to my students. Or, I have had to think as far back as I can to the factors influencing my students' learning—what has shaped them, what will shape them, and how I can work with those factors, and not against them, to help my students succeed both individually and as part of a class (that will expand to include society) when they graduate? How can I teach them to effectively rebel (hold the scissors wrong, but still cut), and what lessons (hidden or as part of the curriculum) are the ones to hang on to, and the ones to let go?

I think it is important when talking about identity: it is that, it's about what I do, and not about me. Yet, in 'doing', I represent the core of who I am, where I'm from, and how I've learned to see the world. Being aware of that and 'doing' in the classroom in a way that helps the students to succeed is why my identity as a teacher is so important. It's also a reason why representation really matters in all schools. The more diverse the teaching staff, the more successful the students.

Q: Has there ever been a time when a teacher or an administrator unfairly questioned the effectiveness of your teaching methods? How did you respond to the teacher or administrator to convince them otherwise?
A: Working abroad is like a continuous exercise in convincing administrators and parents to trust different

teaching methods, but I think this balancing act happens in American schools, too. What I see good teachers do to convince administrators that their methods are effective is to try to reach the goals of the administration and implement their own methods in the classroom. Eventually, trust is established and outcomes are achieved, and administrators grant more latitude. This is only successful if teachers have a clear understanding of what administration goals, priorities, and needs are. And, of course, this becomes more difficult in a system like the UK/US, where the record-keeping (via tests, reports, etc.) overtakes the time saved after trust has been established, meaning that teachers stay on the road to burn-out as a result of overwork. Less effective (and just bad) teachers only do one or the other: meet administration goals or do whatever they want, regardless.

The key word in this question, for me, is "unfairly". Having worked in both administration and teaching, what is 'unfair' looks different to both sides. Administration has a different set of considerations and constraints than an individual classroom teacher, including that of time. So, what may feel "unfair" to a teacher might just be a disconnect or a deficit in understanding on one side or the other. This is where effective school district sensitization comes into play.

Teachers need to understand context and goals, and to know that some parts of these systems won't change. They may need to adapt their methods to make sure some of these needs are met. And sometimes, some teachers who consider themselves effective are just not. Which brings me back around to the balancing act - meeting the goals AND doing one's own thing, even incrementally, until trust is established. I would add that a crucial component of this is consistent, comprehensive communication between administration and staff, both formally through school systems and informally through one-on-one meetings or other means. When administration sees a teacher taking an active role in a school beyond the classroom, that trust is established faster and more solidly.

Q: Any advice you would like to share to help individuals develop their teaching identities?
A: When it comes to interacting with the students, try to go into the classroom without any expectations. The best way to develop your identity as a teacher is through experience. When situations arise, consider carefully how you want to represent yourself in order to create the most open-minded, considered students. That said, how you decorate and organize the classroom, and arrange and present the curricula sets the tone for the year. Be prepared, organized, and have in mind what you want students to learn about the topic and know about you. Sometimes less is better.

$\mathcal{L}$ESSON #5

φ

DETERMINE YOUR WHY

IF YOU ASK A random pool of 100 educators why they decide to pursue a career in teaching, chances are you will receive 100 different responses to that question. Although we, as educators, universally share a love for the youth and developing them into productive citizens in society, the truth is that each of us has personal stories that illustrate our unique motivation for wanting to deeply engage in this important work. We know that individuals do not become teachers because of the money. Actually, most individuals leave the profession altogether because they are severely underpaid by their school district and are not respected for the work they do.

Just this past school year, more than 300 teachers from the Tulsa Public School District in Oklahoma resigned from their positions as a result of their low salaries. In other parts of the state, the narrative is the same. Multiple teachers have been forced to take on second and third jobs in order to supplement their income. According to the U.S. Bureau of Labor and Statistics, Oklahoma teachers had the lowest median salary in the entire nation for the year 2017. For elementary school teachers, their median salary was $38,000 while secondary school teachers earned $40,000. So, if teachers, in general, do not earn livable income wages and do not always earn the respect they deserve from the general public, then why do they continue to remain in the profession?

I discovered my why when I was working at Duckrey. Demographically, Duckrey was similar to most schools within the School District of Philadelphia. Approximately 90 percent of the student body was Black, and the remaining 10 percent was a combination of Asian, Latino, and Native American. It was a Title 1 school, which meant that it was receiving financial assistance from the state of Pennsylvania in order to service the high percentage of students who were coming from low-income families. Like most schools in North Philadelphia, Duckrey had its share of students who fell victim to many of the common social vices that characterize and plague most inner cities in America --

teenage pregnancy, gun violence, drug use, homelessness, and poverty. I witnessed all those things during my time there.

As the school year progressed, I naturally started to observe the dynamics and inner workings of the school. There was one day in particular where I reached an epiphany that would forever change the trajectory of my life. I realized that in almost every classroom, the teacher was white. Now, there were a few Black lead teachers in the building but the overwhelming majority of the staff was white.

How was that the case when approximately 90 percent of the student population was Black? The thought of it really puzzled me and made me wonder why there were so many white teachers and so few Black ones. To delve even deeper into this issue, I also wondered why there were so few Black male teachers in urban schools. It is well documented that Black (and Latino) boys have historically and statistically been the lowest achieving group of students academically throughout the nation.

Many urban school districts have tried to develop initiatives and supports in an effort to close the achievement gap between Black boys and their white counterparts. There are so many factors that have attributed to this achievement gap that I would need to write another book dedicated to that epidemic. The one glaring factor that easily stuck out was the severe lack of Black male representation in the teaching profession. So many Black boys aspire to be professional athletes or music artists because those are the very individuals within the community who represent success and have achieved the status of financial wealth. Also, these professions are exposed to them on a regular basis and presented as the only way to get out of the 'hood' and be successful.

As a Black boy, if I see that the most successful Black men are professional athletes and musical artists, then naturally I'm going to pursue those career paths. What if there were more Black male teachers in our schools and they were held in the same regard as those entertainers? I'm pretty sure more of them would aspire to become educators. A Black male teacher has the power to transform the lives of Black boys in the school system. I wanted to be that difference maker for them. If they were exposed to more Black men who love to teach and want to have a positive impact in the classroom, then maybe they would seriously consider a career in teaching.

At that point, I started to view teaching as a realistic career option. I knew that teaching would place me in a position to nurture my love for children. I could not think of any other job that aligned more perfectly with my passion. Ultimately, I decided to become a teacher because I wanted to show my students, particularly my Black and brown ones, that you can be a successful Black man without having to pursue a professional career in athletics or entertainment.

It took twenty-five years for me to realize that I wanted to become a teacher. I had spent my undergraduate years at Temple as a Mathematics major without having a definitive idea of what I wanted to do for a career. Truthfully, I only chose to major in Mathematics because it was my favorite subject in grade school and I always excelled in it. For educators like former Boston Public Schools history teacher E. Christiaan Summerhill, teaching has always been in his blood. Given his family history, it was inevitable that he would dedicate his life to serving others. A veteran teacher with eleven years of experience, Summerhill reveals his why for becoming an educator:

"I come from a family of educators. My grandparents on both my mother and father's side retired as teachers after 40+ years. This family history makes this question a bit difficult to answer. My first memory of my own teaching came when I moved to Boston at the age of 15. While a student at Dorchester High, my teachers gave me multiple opportunities to 'teach' from facilitating a discussion around Ms. Angelou's 'Caged Bird' to explaining Shakespearean dialogue to my peers.

It was my experience at Dorchester High that motivated me to want to give back to a school system that gave me so much even though I was only a Boston Public Schools (BPS) student for two years. It was those two years that gave me access to a full academic scholarship to the school of my choice. That choice was Morehouse College and that decision changed my life forever.

I also had the opportunity to be a BELL Foundation tutor at a BPS elementary school. It wasn't until I was until I was doing mental health work post-undergrad at a psychiatric hospital that I was convinced to apply to the Boston Teacher Residency Program. I haven't looked back since. My initial impressions were not that teaching was my calling but that service was always something that I enjoyed."

As you evolve as an educator, you may find yourself reshaping your why based on specific experiences you have had in the classroom. Along the way, you will have moments that will question or challenge your perspectives and ideas about education. These moments will not only reshape your why but, consequently, lead to a reshaping of your teaching practices. That turned out to be the case for Marguerite Monahan, a twenty-five-year veteran educator who has worked in multiple school districts throughout the state of Massachusetts. In our interview, she shares a moment during her first year of teaching that forever transformed her thinking around curriculum planning:

> *"In 1989, I was hired as a substitute teacher for the Everett Public Schools, in Everett, MA after I had completed my first year of college. I had teaching practicums during high school, but this was the first opportunity I had to lead a classroom on my own. During my first assignment in a fifth grade classroom, I suggested to the students that they try to complete the assignment that was left for them so that they would have less to finish for homework. The students began a conversation with me that stayed with me for the rest of my teaching career.*
>
> *I was informed by the surprisingly respectful and eloquent fifth graders, that their teacher was not allowed to assign homework without getting administrative approval. They told me that over the course of the year, homework had been used as a punishment tool, so much so that the parents had to intervene and a policy for just this teacher had to be put in place. Over the course of my undergraduate studies, where I had the opportunity to create assessments, lesson plans, and homework assignments, I would think back on that experience and use it to guide me to try to create and assign meaningful work for my students."*

In the end, our core values and principles as educators must align with our why. The road to being a great educator is one that can only be travelled by a special individual. As you hit those potholes and speed bumps, remember that your momentum will push you forward. Your why is your momentum and point of reference when you need to re-center yourself. Without that why, your engine will break down and never recover.

SUMMARY

Before you decide to pursue a career as a teacher, you have to determine your why. You need to determine your reason for wanting to pursue this important work. You can't go into the teaching profession not knowing why you want to do it. Your why should serve as the foundation of your identity as a teacher. It should be the main reason why you arrive at school early in the morning to make photocopies of worksheets and organize your classroom before the arrival of your students.

Your why should be the reason why you spend countless hours outside of the school building, creating weekly lesson plans, grading papers, and making phone calls to parents to update them on their child's academic progress. Your why should also be the reason why you have the strength and determination to keep coming back to the classroom after a rough day with the students. Your why is the fuel to your engine and the cleanser of your spirit when feelings of indifference and despair attempt to creep into your soul. Your why is what allows your heart to remain open to your students, even when they do everything in their power to test your will.

If you are not sure what your why is, it is in your best interest to take some time to think about that. Here are a few tips that will guide you in solidifying your why:

1. Identify your potential strengths as a teacher

Each of us is blessed with talents and abilities that can make the world a better place. In order to capitalize on your strengths, you must first identify what they are. Below are a few questions you can ask yourself to pinpoint your strengths:

- *What natural abilities do you possess?*
- *What actions allow you to get a positive response from the people you respect?*
- *What are your dominant gifts?*

The best way to define your strengths is to interview your friends and family. It is best to interview them because they know you better than anyone else. When conducting the interviews, be sure to keep a running record of your responses. Try to interview at least 10 people so that you have a sufficient amount of responses to review. As you are reviewing the responses, highlight any noticeable trends in the data. These findings will bring you one step closer to recognizing your potential as a teacher.

2. Define your mission as an educator

It is impossible to be an effective teacher if you lack an emotional connection to this work. The best teachers exude a passion that empowers them to be quality role models for their students. Your passion stems from your personal morals, beliefs, and values. Some of us can point to a particular moment in our life that ignited our love for teaching while others need more time to flesh out their thoughts. If you are in the latter group, the following questions will help define your passion:

- *What motivates you when you are most productive?*
- *What grieves your heart and infuriates you the most?*
- *What do you do that makes you feel good emotionally and spiritually?*
- *What makes you passionate about teaching?*
- *What difference do you want to make in the lives of your students?*
- *What type of impact do you want to make in the field of education?*

Your responses to these questions may reveal the underlining issues that are the driving force for your mission as an educator. As long as passion is at the core of your character, you will maintain the determination to fulfill your mission. Teaching is far from being the most lucrative career out there and the majority of people who get into this profession do it because they genuinely want to positively impact the lives of young children. You cannot be an effective teacher, especially within an urban school, if you do not have a personal connection to this work. If you view teaching as a job, then you should consider pursuing a different career path.

IDENTITY TALK
WITH AN EDUCATOR

———

Sherna Spearman-Lott is the first grade inclusion teacher at Martha Rawls Smith Elementary school, which is part of the Wayne County School District in Jesup, GA. A veteran teacher with nineteen years of experience, Sherna serves as the mentor teacher for all the first year teachers within her school, in addition to occupying a multitude of leadership roles within her school district. In this interview, Sherna shares what led her down the path of becoming a teacher and highlights the educators who have played a significant role in her evolution as an educator.

Q: Why did you want to become a teacher? Was there a particular moment in your life that motivated you to pursue this career path?

A: Growing up in rural GA, I rarely encountered teachers that looked like me in the classroom! I didn't grow up in the South that most people think of Atlanta. My town's racial makeup is predominantly white. Blacks only represent about 25% of the population. I always thought I'd go to college and become a lawyer like Claire Huxtable, but one day that dream just changed!

I set my sights on becoming a teacher and never looked back! I knew I was pretty smart growing up, but I am extra thankful to teachers like Mrs. Sarah Paul who showed a special interest in a little girl that looked nothing like her and encouraged me to do more! I recall the day that Angie Anderson shared a Christmas ornament with me that still hangs on my family tree each year (Angie and I are now co-workers and she's had the pleasure of teaching both of my kids in the gifted program.)

I recall sitting in Mrs. Linda Marcus' eighth grade science class and listening to her speak with so much passion about her area of study. I vividly flashback to Mrs. Linda Lockley-Kelly's history class and the heated debates she would facilitate between students. We felt safe to express our views, and we knew that she would provide us with facts to support or disprove our naivety.

I also have fond memories of my best friend's mom, Mrs. Peggy Riggins, and her senior Psychology Class. I think she may have brainwashed us all because learning about countless men from around the globe was actually fascinating! I cannot leave out Mrs. Jamie Denty because her back to back Literature classes almost caused me to hate reading for fun and writing, in general. However, succeeding in her classes assured me that I was prepared for what's next in college! Most of these teachers were not of color, but I bet you will have a difficult time figuring out who's who because their love for my education knew no color!

Q: Who is/are your personal mentor(s) in the field of education? In what ways have they supported your growth as an educator?

A: I currently serve as a mentor teacher for first-year teachers in my school, but I cannot recall ever being assigned a mentor teacher! My experience as a mentor allows me to provide guidance and encouragement that I could have benefited from early on in my career. I get to see firsthand how a strong support system can cause a teacher to not give up in our profession. I have also seen the negative results of poor/non-existent support. These poor teachers usually leave the school or the profession altogether. No one wins in this instance!

I did adopt a neighboring teacher, in my 5th year of teaching, as a mentor. Mrs. Alice Kicklighter was late in her career when she crossed my path, but she still exhibited an enthusiasm for teaching small children and that was magical! I would listen to her calm tone in the hallway, and I would find myself visiting her classroom for ideas on a weekly basis. My daughter would also come home with a new story about The Learning Lady every afternoon. I knew that I wanted to leave a similar positive impression on my young learners. I may not maintain a calm tone or low volume, however, I do feel that my students leave my classroom but never leave my influence! In this community, I have the pleasure of watching my babies grow into young adults. Many of them come back to visit over the years, and high school graduation invitations greet me each Spring!

Q: Who was your favorite teacher growing up? What important life lessons did this individual teach you? How has this individual influenced your teaching style?
A: I can recall a Black paraprofessional sprinkled throughout elementary grades, but the day I met Mrs. Merritt changed my ideals about learning and school! She had such high expectations for her students, and she truly believed in consequences. I had to rein in my high energy and smart mouth because she demanded respect! I also knew that Mrs. Merritt knew where I lived, and that fear was amplified when she ran into my mom around town. As an educator, I realize that Mrs. Merritt kept her students in line with tough love and genuine concern for our well-being/outcome! In my classroom, I started the year off by building relationships with my students through clear expectations, consistency, and an interest in who they are inside and outside of school. I make certain that parents know that they can count on me

as I will depend on them to reinforce skills taught on a daily basis.

Q: Any advice you would like to share to help individuals develop their teaching identities?

A: I recently shared some advice with my assistant principal from last year (now a principal at her own school) on how to deal with a past student. I told her that this girl is keenly aware when she is loved versus when she is simply being tolerated. Her new teacher needs to be confident enough to push her, but the teacher cannot hold a grudge from day to day. Every child (and a lot of adults) could benefit from a fresh start! I shared that my success with the little girl which was a direct result of relationship building and understanding personalities.

A teacher's success in a classroom requires getting to know oneself as much as getting to know the students! More than anything, memories from my childhood and early on in my career helped me to continually develop my teaching style. Everything will not work with every child! There is no magic formula for teaching! Approach each day ready to give and receive! Remember to just BE... Be Positive! Be Encouraging! Be Supportive! Be a High Achiever! (But don't get discouraged by some lows), and Be ready for each day with a smile and renewed energy!

$\mathcal{L}$ESSON #6

φ

MENTORS ARE YOUR LIFELINE

TEACHING IS ONE OF the rewarding careers to have but it is also one of the most difficult. There are so many things for which a teacher is responsible. Let's start with the process of acquiring a teaching license. Before you can even be hired to teach at a school, you have to pass a series of certification tests in the content area you want to teach and obtain a Master's degree in Education. Although teaching licensure guidelines are slightly varied between the different states, the process of acquiring one is practically the same. Even after you receive it, there are so many more things you need to learn.

Outside of providing academic instruction and managing the behaviors of students, you have to demonstrate the ability to plan effective lessons, grade student assignments, learn the academic standards of your content area, and build relationships with your students' families so that they are kept abreast of how their children are performing academically. Even after you get a few years of teaching under your belt, you still have to earn a certain number of continuing education credits in order to keep your teaching license active and advance to the next certification level. This involves participating in professional development workshops outside of school hours and completing post-graduate courses within the content area of your teaching license.

In recognizing the need for improved teacher education, many school districts across the nation have created teacher induction programs to support new educators entering the field. Many of these programs operate under the umbrella of the New Teacher Center (NTC), a national non-profit organization whose mission is to enhance the quality of student learning by strengthening the practice of beginning teachers. As of 2017, thirty-one states have officially joined the NTC network and have adopted new teacher induction policies that align with the organization's mission.

Consequently, NTC-supported school districts have witnessed a significant increase in teacher retention and gains in student learning. In Florida, the Hillsborough County Public Schools District saw a 31% increase in teacher retention after two years of NTC support. Due to this increase, the district was able to save and invest their money on other important educational resources. Hillsborough County is just one of the many school districts whose educators have greatly benefited from on-the-job mentoring.

Given everything that I have just mentioned, it is abundantly clear that the tedious nature of this profession warrants the need for guidance and support. Regardless of what stage you are in your career, it is imperative that you surround yourself with individuals who are experienced and have a proven track record in the profession. Looking back at my own journey, I have been guided by many mentors but none have been more impactful to my growth as an educator than Salome Thomas-EL.

Salome Thomas-EL was the principal at Russell Byers Charter School in Philadelphia, PA when I started there ten years ago. From what I remember, Principal EL was loved and revered by many of the teachers and all of the students. He brought a sense of swag that permeated throughout the school and gave you a reason to want to come to work every day. He wasn't that principal who spent 90% of his time in his office doing paperwork and isolating himself from the kids. He was omnipresent in every sense of the word. There was not a day that went by where he wasn't actively engaged with the students.

Being that he was a former math teacher, Principal EL could relate to the rigors that come with teaching. He was still a teacher at heart who relished the opportunities to make surprise classroom visits and engage the kids in an old-school rap or a mini-Algebra lesson. Just when you thought he couldn't be any more amazing, he ran an after-school chess club. When I say he ran it, he approached it with the same level of passion that he did with every other aspect of the school day. Under his leadership, Russell Byers developed into a formidable chess team that won national chess championships. Principal EL was the ultimate leader and the students loved him!

Throughout that first year, Principal EL served as my advocate and mentor. He took me under his wing and treated me like his son. He was never shy about stating the need for more Black men to pursue a career in teaching in the inner city. He knew first-hand how the presence of a Black male teacher could have a positive and lasting impact on a young child aspiring to transcend their personal obstacles and chase their dreams. I honestly believe that was why Principal EL took a vested interest in advancing my career. I think he saw a lot of himself in me. Sadly, Black male teachers have historically been the anomalies in the American school system, so when a school administrator comes across a Black man who even has the slightest interest in teaching, he or she will do everything possible to empower and mold that person into a great educator.

Principal EL would end up teaching me many lessons about being a professional. For instance, he noticed that I was leaving work immediately after the students dismissed. This troubled him because most of the teachers were logging 10 to 12 hour work days and he felt acquiring this habit would be a golden opportunity for me to show teachers that I was serious about being a teacher. By staying after school and working into the early evening hours, it showed that I was a team player and committed to upholding the school's reputation as a high performing school.

When Principal EL always reiterated that teachers needed to put in the time and effort now in order to capture all aspects of the job. In order for that to happen, he stressed the need for me to find my niche within the school. Finding my niche meant identifying a need within the school and figuring out a creative way to satisfy the said need. This would allow me to be more visible to the school community. He suggested that I create a bulletin board that recognized individual sixth-grade students who were making strides academically and behaviorally throughout the month. This bulletin board would be my niche – the one project of which I had complete ownership.

So, I took his advice and created the bulletin board, which was located directly across from the sixth grade classrooms. I titled the bulletin board, "Who's Got It Made In 6th Grade?" The title was inspired by the rapper Special Ed's hit song, *I Got It Made*. I Got It Made was Special Ed's ode to his self-proclaimed dopeness. Throughout the song, he brags about his Caribbean heritage, his love for girls, his financial exploits, and, of course, his lyrical ability. I wanted this bulletin board to embody the swagger and sense of cool that the song exuded.

One of Principal EL's popular sayings was that "every child deserves to have someone to be crazy about them." The "Who Got It Made in 6th Grade?" would be my special way of celebrating the scholarly achievements of the students. At the end of every month, I selected four students – two boys and two girls. I would take their pictures and post them up on the bulletin board with their full names. Their faces would stay on the board for the entire month before being replaced by another lucky group of students. This board lived for the remainder of the school year and it was a huge hit with the students! It got to the point where students were approaching me asking, "Mr. Sarfo-Mensah, can I be on the board for this month?" The students took tremendous pride in being publicly recognized for their achievements in the classroom.

Another important lesson that Principal EL taught me was the importance of dressing in a professional manner. His belief was that dressing professionally reinforced to students that school is a place of business. Wearing a shirt and tie was a non-verbal way of letting students know that you, the teacher, were seriously committed to the challenge of pushing them to reach their potential academically and behaviorally. In the spirit of that philosophy, all staff members at Russell Byers had to adhere to the business casual dress code.

On a personal level, dressing up brought out a sense of coolness and swag that I yearned to have during my elementary school years. It gave me the energy and motivation I needed to perform at a high level. Simply put, when you look good, you feel good. And if I feel good about myself and what I'm wearing, I will have the energy and motivation I need to be the best teacher for my students. The more productive I was at work, the more I subscribed to that very notion.

My first year at Russell Byers would end up being Principal EL's final year at the school. He accepted an offer to become the new principal of Thomas Edison Charter School in Wilmington, DE. It was a great opportunity for him but selfishly, I wanted him to stay. He was a major reason why I decided to join the staff at Russell Byers. I personally was looking forward to working under his leadership for many more years.

In the one year we worked together, I learned more about teaching and being a professional from him than I did at my first two schools. I thought that I would have more time to absorb more knowledge from him. Nevertheless, I was thankful that he, at least, provided me with the necessary tools to navigate a professional workplace like Russell Byers. Even though he was moving on to a new school, I still had his many gems of wisdom to lean on moving forward.

Unfortunately, there are certain educators who have gone their entire teaching careers without having an official mentor. However, they have been able to fill that void by surrounding themselves with a support group of educators. Erica Mason shares how the power of sharing best teaching practices can help educators strengthen their craft:

"One of the things that has always bothered me about my teaching career is that I never had a mentor. For my practicums, I was assigned old teachers in Boston Public Schools who were past burnout and should have been encouraged to move into other roles long before I met them. They also were not particularly great at mentoring a young, strong, woman.

I have taught primarily in cultural environments that were different to the ones in which I grew up, and I really craved someone who could guide me and my choices. I made a lot of mistakes on my journey to teaching excellence, and while I learned from them, I also felt that many choices were failures. In fact, one of the best lessons you can learn from a mentor is that those failures are a necessary component of reflective teaching and that we can grow and become stronger from them. I would have been happy to have had a mentor tell me that, and so I have really tried to be present for new teachers in that way.

My co-teachers have been a great source of learning for me at every stage of my career. When I started teaching, I was very young, and the teachers I worked with gave me great curriculum ideas, supported me, and helped me learn the importance of preparation and consistent classroom management. As I grew, I found that teachers were strengthened, not threatened, by sharing, and I made that a regular component of the curricula when I conducted teacher trainings."

A school community is always stronger when all the teachers are working together to make each other better. The best schools are successful because they function within a culture of collegiality and collaboration. Within this type of environment, students are at the forefront. Even if you are a strong teacher and you are excelling at your job, none of that matters if your school, as a whole, is not succeeding. Humility allows us to develop a growth mindset, which consequently enables us to provide support to those who are motivated and interested in building their capacity as classroom facilitators. Sometimes, we find mentors who are outside of our school community. This was the case for Erica Jones, who explains how a distinguished collection of women supported her growth as an educator:

"I was blessed to serve as a committee co-chair for a phenomenal organization called Black Women's Educational Alliance (BWEA). Within this organization, I found a plethora of women whom I cherished as personal resources. I counted on them for guidance, motivation, and accountability. These women consisted of principals, teachers, and assistant superintendents who understood the plight of Black educators.

More importantly, they understood the urgency in improving the education conditions for our youth and the unity amongst each other that is needed to do so. I recommend anyone in the field of teaching to start a support circle of educators in various positions. Meet and talk with them regularly using a receiving ear. My sister circle truly saved me several times."

Whether or not your mentor is someone within your school, be sure that the people who you assign as mentors are individuals who have invested in your professional growth and are committed to supporting you in every phase of your career. The journey to becoming an effective educator is one that you should not embark on alone. The journey is always sweeter when you are in the company of dreamers, motivators, spiritual elevators, and accountability partners. Mentors are valuable resources so take full advantage of them while they are around.

SUMMARY

Mentorship is necessary in order to navigate the many rigors of teaching. Your mentor can be a classroom teacher, an administrator, or an experienced support staff member. Mentors are essential to a teacher's progression because they provide direction and encouragement in times when you feel lost. They can also help to create opportunities for career advancement by connecting you with individuals who are in educational leadership and provide helpful tips that you can use to improve your instructional practices. I would not be where I am today if it wasn't for the mentorship of the many teachers, former principals, and support staff members in the different schools where I have worked.

The greatest evidence of the mentorship I have received throughout my career is my teaching style, which is basically a blend of recycled instructional strategies and methods I have acquired from the different teachers I have supported over the years. In order to have longevity in this profession, you need to build a support system of trusted individuals who will advocate for you and support you every step of the way. When selecting a mentor, you should strongly consider the following criteria:

1. Mentors should be open to sharing their knowledge and expertise on teaching. For that reason, you should take full advantage of your time with your mentor and ask as many questions as possible.

2. Mentors should be passionate about their work as educators. They should approach their daily work with a positive attitude and believe that every day is an opportunity to grow personally and professionally.

3. Mentors firmly believe that developing into a quality educator is a continuous process. They should actively participate in professional development workshops and engage in educational literature that builds their intellectual capacity.

4. Mentors should assist teachers in creating ongoing personal and professional goals. They also frequently check in with teachers to evaluate how much progress they have made towards achieving their goals.

5. Mentors should provide guidance and constructive feedback to teachers. They should openly identify your strengths and weaknesses as a teacher in order to provide strategies that will foster growth in your instructional practices.

IDENTITY TALK
WITH AN EDUCATOR

―――――

Dr. Johni Cruse Craig currently serves as the National project director for two educational programs (Delta Teacher Efficacy Campaign – DTEC and Teacher Advocating to lead Great change – T.A.G.) of the Delta Research and Educational Foundation in collaboration with Delta Sigma Theta Sorority, Incorporated.

Throughout her twenty-two year career as an educator, Johni has worked as a science and mathematics teacher in various middle schools throughout the states of North Carolina and Georgia. She is also the founder and CEO of Heart 2 Heart Services, a non-profit organization that provides educational consultation, coaching, and motivational speaker services. Johni identifies the multiple mentors who have supported her growth as an educator.

Q: Who was your favorite teacher growing up? What important life lessons did this individual teach you? How has this individual influenced your teaching style?

A: I had several - Mrs. Mingo - my first grade teacher because she advocated for me all while paddling me with love to make sure I remained focused and obedient. My eighth grade science teacher, Ms. Jones, as she pushed me to perform at my full potential with her expectations and rigor. She did not give grades, they were earned and I had to buckle down to maintain an A/B as a C was not an option in my home. Lastly, my Mom was my first teacher as she stayed home with me for the first 3 years of my life and created a learning environment where I thrived in reading, writing, and arithmetic before entering the head start program.

Q: Who is/are your personal mentor(s) in the field of education? In what ways have they supported your growth as an educator?

A: Dr. Vernice Loveless: My college professor and mentor to this day. She helped shape my mind around best practices for lessons and a deep knowledge of interdisciplinary lessons. Matthew Priester: He was the principal who assigned me many leadership roles in the school and district and allowed me to learn, create, plan and execute many activities for school improvement and professional development.

Ms. Roslyn Stewart: I hired her as a science teacher and we began mentoring each other. She continues to stretch me spiritually and professionally as it relates to best practices in teaching Science.

Ms. Cathy Goolsby: She was an amazing instructional coach and support when I transitioned schools and had a class with resource and gifted students. She was very supportive of the innovative ideas in the classroom and resourceful when assistance was needed to get materials for different hands-on activities. I learned great collaboration skills under her guidance.

Each of them supported my growth and equipped me for the present tasks.

Q: Any advice you would like to share to help individuals develop their teaching identities?

A: It is HEART work. Check your motives and WHY and if they ever dwindle and are not easily re-anchored...seek some professional development and a community that can support and inspire you or maybe it is time to walk away to eliminate further damaging students. That is the hard truth. When you look at it from that perspective, it simplifies what the next step should be.

$\mathcal{L}$ESSON #7

φ

YOU ARE YOUR
#1 ADVOCATE

IN THE PREVIOUS CHAPTER, I discussed the importance of having mentors in your support circle. As important as mentors are to a teacher's growth process, their presence means absolutely nothing if the teacher continues to lack trust and confidence in their teaching abilities. Teaching has a way of tapping into strengths and qualities that you didn't even realize you possessed. It also forces you to find your voice and make it heard when others try to control your narrative. When you consider the level of investment and commitment that is required to be the best teacher to your students, it warrants the need for you to protect your reputation at all costs.

Unfortunately, there have been a few instances in my career where colleagues have made false claims about my abilities as a teacher without even taking the time to visit my classroom and have a direct conversation with me. When my principal brought the issue to my attention, I simply presented to her a documentation of student test scores and work samples that reflected the amount of growth that my students have achieved under my watch. Once I did that, the issue was put to rest. It doesn't matter how many years you have been in the teaching game. Even if you are a first-year teacher, understand that there is power in your words and that you have the right to professionally defend yourself when certain colleagues are out to defame your character.

Ageism is highly prevalent in the world of teaching. The most popular case of this is when the twenty-year veteran teacher is dictating to a young teacher the manner in which they should teach instead of giving them the space to develop their own teacher voice. The young teacher may disagree with the veteran teacher's motives but they fail to respond back because of their perceived status within the pecking order of teachers in the school. Veteran teachers are a premium to have at any school because they can provide helpful insight and experience that can help younger teachers.

However, simply accumulating many years of teaching does not automatically make them more effective teachers than those who are still in the early stages of their careers. For that reason, young teachers should trust their instincts and not feel shy about professionally pushing back at veteran teachers. Even though veteran teachers act with the best of intentions, they can sometimes cripple your development as a teacher without even realizing it.

The same can be said about administrators who have logged many years as an educator. During the summer after my first year of teaching, I was searching for a new teaching home for the upcoming school year. I would end up interviewing at four different schools during that summer but there was one interview in particular that really left a sour taste in my mouth.

THE INTERVIEW FROM HELL

This interview took place at Bowman Prep Charter School, which was located in the northeastern section of Philadelphia. I did not know much about the school other than the fact that it was located in the heart of one of the rougher neighborhoods in the city. Sadly, I was in for a rude awakening. When I arrived at the school for my interview, I reported to the main office and the school secretary escorted me to another classroom where the principal was waiting.

For the sake of anonymity, I will refer to the principal as "Dr. Dick". After a quick exchange of pleasantries, I handed my resume to Dr. Dick. According to him, most Black male teachers he had interviewed in the past were underprepared and did not have their teacher certification. He was immediately impressed that I was a young Black man who already had his teaching certification and was seriously committed to the profession. He was even more impressed when he saw that I taught at Russell Byers.

At the back of my mind, I thought this interview would be smooth sailing but then, the interview took a turn for the worst. Given Russell Byers' reputation for being one of the premier schools in Philadelphia, he was surprised that I was no longer working there. When he asked why I left, I didn't hold back the truth. I told him I was let go because my students performed poorly on the Pennsylvania System of School Assessment (PSSA). As soon as he heard that, he immediately became irate and began to question my integrity as a teacher. Quite frankly, his tone went from being cordial to utterly disrespectful in a matter of seconds. His behavior and lack of professionalism was unbecoming of a school leader who was well respected in his many education circles. He wondered how he could trust me to raise the PSSA scores of sixth-grade students at Bowman when I couldn't accomplish that at Russell Byers.

In response, I asserted that the lack of instructional support from the school's leadership team played a significant role in my failures. That statement just infuriated him even more. He then went on a profanity-laced rant about how he, as a first-year teacher, had very little resources at his disposal but managed to find a way to figure it out. He also pointed out that he did this in an era where there was no advanced technology.

At this point of the interview, I was resigned to the reality that I wasn't going to get the sixth grade teaching position and it was also clear that he was totally disgusted by me. Just when I thought my spirit couldn't be crushed any more, he mentioned that he would possibly consider me for the vacant second grade teaching position. By placing me in that position, he believed that it would be a learning opportunity for me to sharpen my teaching skills. He also wasn't shy in admitting that this would prevent me from bringing down the school's overall PSSA test scores.

Considering that Bowman had been underachieving academically for a number of years and was in danger of being taken over by the state, it was somewhat understandable that Dr. Dick sadly perceived me as a liability rather than an asset. To end the interview, he insisted that I go home and email him a short letter explaining why he should seriously consider me for the second grade teaching position. Later that day, I stood in front of my laptop, contemplating on how to respond to Dr. Dick's job offer. Honestly, I had no desire of teaching second grade but the pressures of maintaining a stable income to keep up with my living expenses forced me to give his offer some consideration.

In my heart, I believed that I was a good teacher with the potential of being even better. All I needed was for one school to give me an opportunity to showcase what I can do. I also needed that school to believe that I could be a valuable contributor to whatever they were trying to accomplish. That being said, I realized that Bowman would not be the right fit for me. By declining the job offer, I exercised self-advocacy by deciding that I was not going to subject myself to the verbal and emotional abuse of a school leader who had no intentions of helping me develop as an educator. As tempted as I was to accept the offer, I ultimately decided against it because I recognized that working under Dr. Dick would have a crippling effect on my development as a teacher. He already made it clear that he lacked confidence in my teaching abilities and that was enough for me to look elsewhere.

Throughout the making of this book, almost every educator I interviewed expressed that they had been through situations where they had to justify their teaching methods after being confronted by their school leaders or colleagues. Although their situations differed from each other, they were all able to provide convincing evidence that substantiated their classroom success. Shirley Jones-Luke, an English-Language Arts teacher at McCormack Middle

School in Boston, recounted how she stayed true to her teaching methods in the face of opposition during her early teaching years:

"I never doubted my abilities. I came from a family that valued education. I wanted to give back to my community and help students of color become better readers, writers, and thinkers. I had a mentor at Madison (Park Technical High School) who helped me create lessons and gave me classroom management tips. I had some students who would challenge me almost every day, driving other teachers out of the school. I was determined to stay. I would not be driven away. Administrators didn't like my teaching style or my relationship with students. But I did everything they asked and it was never satisfactory.

However, my students at Madison were the results that could not be denied. I turned resistant readers into public speakers. I turned students into poets. I showed my colleagues and administrators that my teaching was effective as many of my students went on to graduate with honors and moved onto higher education."

What Shirley describes is a situation that happens way too often with teachers. School leaders and administrators have their own perspectives of what quality instruction should look like based on their experiences in the classroom. Sometimes, those perspectives do not align with the ones their teachers have. As a result, tension builds up between the teacher and the administrator as they are trying to convince each other that their teaching approach will produce the best results for student success.

From the teacher's point of view, they believe that they know what's best for their students because they spend more time with them than anyone else. In some cases, the administrator may suggest a teaching strategy or a resource for the teacher to try out. In the end, Johnny Ray James II, the Director of Extended Learning at KIPP Charter School in New Jersey, said it best: "Let the numbers talk for me, and let the students speak on behalf of themselves." Data will always silence administrators and colleagues because of its objective nature. If you are able to validate your methods with data, administrators and colleagues will be more inclined to trust your judgment. Remember, any data that makes the school look good, makes the school administrators look good.

SUMMARY

When times are tough and the naysayers are chirping, remind yourself that you are a person of value who is capable of being an asset to any school that decides to invest in you. Self-confidence is an attractive quality to school administrators and other teachers. When school administrators are making a decision on whether to hire you for a teaching position at their school, you have to sell them on your merit. Get them to envision how much better their school will be if they bring you onto their team. If an administrator senses that you have doubt or a lack of confidence in your ability to carry out the responsibilities of the job for which you are interviewing, that is enough for them to pass on you and look at other potential candidates. If you don't believe in yourself, who will?

Finally, always remember that you have the power to control your narrative. The classroom is your domain and you ultimately have the license to operate it however you see fit for your students. There will always be that one teacher or administrator who questions your motives. Don't be afraid to professionally speak your mind and communicate to them your perspectives and rationale behind the instructional decisions you make within your classroom. Oftentimes, a well-thought-out and clearly articulated rationale is all that an administrator needs to give you the freedom to do your thing.

IDENTITY TALK
WITH AN EDUCATOR

————

Dre Cleveland is the founder & CEO of Tru Transformation Coaching, LLC, a New-York based company that is dedicated to empowering the urban community through live and online seminars, workshops, events, organizational training, and personal coaching. A former elementary school teacher within the New York City Public School System, Dre has first-hand knowledge of the social and emotional barriers that many students face in their development as scholars. In this interview, she shares about how she was able to persevere and overcome some of the most challenging moments of her career.

Q: Describe your earliest introduction to teaching. What type of work were you doing? What were your initial impressions?

A: My first introduction to teaching was as a teaching assistant at Cornell University, at one of the schools in downtown Ithaca. I worked with second graders on building literacy and a love for reading. That was the first time I really realized the impact a teacher has on students. I was only 19 years old, but that impression stuck with me. Even though I was in school for child psychology, I truly believe that is what swayed my decision to stay in education.

Q: Has there ever been a time when a teacher or an administrator unfairly questioned the effectiveness of your teaching methods? How did you respond to the teacher or administrator to convince them otherwise?

A: Yes. At the beginning of my career, I had an administrator that reminded me of Cruella De Vil (from the Disney film, "101 Dalmatians"). Nothing I did was right to her. Everything was either incorrectly done, or I was threatened with her reasons why my students wouldn't pass their state tests because I wasn't "executing the curriculum correctly." The strange thing was that I was in my Master's program, and most of the techniques I was using came directly from there!

I cried a lot that year, and I seriously thought about not continuing to teach. I almost let her negativity get the best of me, but I chose to allow the response I got from my students and my parents to lead me. My students did excellent work that year, and quite a few of my parents let me know that their children were eager to do their work at home, something they struggled with in the past. I learned to focus there instead of letting the opinion of others deter me - even if it was an evil supervisor.

Q: Describe a moment in your teaching career when you faced a major challenge. What specific lesson did you learn from that challenge and how did it help support your growth as an educator?

A: My biggest challenge was during my third year teaching fifth grade in a school in Brownsville. I had what was supposed to be the "bottom class," full of students who belonged in either sixth or seventh grade. The issue was that the students were used to being treated the way teachers generally treat the "bottom kids." They had perfected that reflection of themselves and acted accordingly. That is what I walked into that year. Those children literally tried to run me out of the classroom, and I almost let them.

At that point, I decided to help them change the way they saw themselves and the way that I saw them. At that point, we created magic, and that "bottom class" became my top class and proved what they were really capable of on their state tests and beyond. That year really catapulted my passion for changing the way education is done, from the inside out. That year, I learned that the main ingredient in producing high performance in ANY student is working on their self-image and belief in themselves along with how you as the educator see them as well. They are the reason I do what I do today as an educational consultant and life coach.

Q: Any other advice you would like to share to help individuals develop their teaching identities?

A: The main advice I would give to any educator is to understand yourself as a physician of sorts. The biggest transformations you will see in your students begin with how you operate on their inside. Your work will show on the outside in what they produce in your classroom, but it starts from within. I don't think schools focus enough attention on professional development for the inner work that needs to be done to create the results you truly want to produce in ANY classroom...with ANY students. Do yourself the favor of investing in your own personal development, so that you can be a catalyst for transformation for all of your students...especially the students that need you the most.

$\mathcal{L}$ESSON #8

φ

CULTURAL RESPONSIVENESS IS A REQUIREMENT FOR RELATIONSHIP BUILDING

EARLIER IN THE BOOK, I stated that I ultimately wanted to become a teacher because I was disheartened by the fact that there were so few male teachers of color within the profession. This issue is most prevalent in urban school districts all across this nation. I first witnessed this during my time at Duckrey. When I worked there, a majority of the teachers were white and yet, Blacks and Latinos accounted for the vast majority of the student population.

In my observations, I identified three types of white teachers: the Champion, the Apprentice and the Oppressor.

The Champion clearly had close relationships with the students and created a safe positive classroom climate that allowed for meaningful learning to take place. The Apprentice genuinely had the best of intentions but struggled mightily to connect with the students and that ultimately led to a destructive cycle of classroom chaos, which made it practically impossible to teach. Finally, the Oppressor simply went through the motions and made it clear that they weren't truly interested in helping their students succeed because they inherently subscribed to the negative stereotypes spewed out about Blacks and Latinos being incapable of conducting themselves appropriately and performing at a high level academically. So, here's the question. What separates the first type of white teacher from the other two? The answer is cultural competence.

Depending on what literary source you read, you may encounter a slightly different definition of what cultural competence is. The American Psychological Association loosely defines the term as "the ability to understand, appreciate and interact with people from cultures or belief systems different from one's own". According to the National Education Association, it is defined as "having an awareness of one's own cultural identity and views about the difference, and the ability to learn and build on the varying cultural and community norms of students and their families". In the health care world, cultural competence is "the ability of providers and organizations to effectively deliver health care services that meet the social, cultural, and linguistic needs of patients".

Regardless of what definition you find, it is clear that cultural competence is a necessary skill to have in order to build healthy relationships with other human beings. In the context of urban education, there is no way that a teacher can effectively create a structured classroom learning environment without mastering this skill.

Just to be clear, cultural competency is not just applicable to relationships between Black people and white people. It is a required skill to have when people from different parts of the African Diaspora interact with one another. This can also be said about Asian, Latin American, Native American, and all other cultures, as there are several nationalities that fall within each of those ethnic groups. In my case, my current school has a student population that is predominantly Black and Latino.

Within each of those races, there are a number of cultural differences for which I need take into account. For instance, majority of the Black students at my school are of Caribbean descent but then there is another group of Black students who have no ancestral ties to the Caribbean islands. Those distinctions alone warrant the need for teachers to be culturally competent. Furthermore, developing cultural competence as an educator will help you in forging strong relationships with your students.

By normalizing the habit of grounding your instructional practices within the cultural contexts of your students, you will succeed in creating academic lessons and learning tasks that will invite students to use their culture as a tool to make meaningful connections to the content they are being taught. Simply put, the merging of cultural competence with academic curricula gives birth to culturally responsive teaching. The concept of culturally responsive teaching is not as complex as it appears. As educators, we are taught to adjust our instructional practice to meet the learning needs of our students.

Culturally responsive teaching is basically a method of scaffolding. Essentially, we are designing lessons and tailoring our instruction in a manner that enables students to utilize their cultural literacy as a scaffold to master desired learning objectives. More than ever, teachers need to develop a pedagogical toolbox that will equip them to be proficient facilitators in a multi-cultural classroom.

ELIMINATING THE WHITE SAVIOR COMPLEX

In urban schools, there are certain white teachers who possess the "white savior complex". In other words, they subscribe to the popular notion that they are the answer to saving their Black and Latino students from the perils of society. They spend more time being apologists for the plight of their Black and Latino students than teaching them how to be accountable for their learning. Fortunately, I have had the pleasure of working with white teachers who did not subscribe to that mindset. Elizabeth DiFranco and Lily Allison are two teachers who truly exemplify what it means to be a culturally responsive educator.

Elizabeth teaches seventh and eighth English Language Arts and has been my grade-level partner teacher throughout my time at the Joseph Lee School. Lily and I worked together for three years at Killissac Charter School. Currently, she works as a kindergarten teacher at Ellington Elementary School in Philadelphia. Throughout their careers, both women have consistently supplemented the Language Arts curriculum with novels and literary selections primarily focused on people of color. Through their efforts, their students have learned how to appreciate and understand cultures that are different from their own.

Although they are cognizant of the obstacles that their students face outside of school and show empathy towards their plight, they never allow them to use their personal situations as excuses for not being able to fulfill their academic expectations. Rather, they empower them to use their plight as a motivation to transcend their obstacles and excel in the classroom.

In our recent conversation, Elizabeth and Lily both reveal the learning process they have undergone to develop into culturally responsive teachers in an urban school setting.

They also provided their analysis of the 'white savior' complex and described how that impacts the manner in which white teachers teach students of color.

Q: What challenges have you both had to overcome being white teachers at schools where the student population is predominantly people of color? Do you believe that your "whiteness" has had an impact on your ability to teach your students and interact with Black staff members & parents?

Elizabeth DiFranco: Biggest challenge – trust. I cannot pretend that I understand what it is to be a Black person. I can't and don't. The only aspect I can relate to is poverty. I am a product of the welfare system and have an intimate knowledge of fear, hunger, and judgement based on my economic status. However, the inequities that face individuals of color are aspects of life that I continue to learn every day.

My hope is that I continue to live an honest life as a compassionate, tolerant activist. I want my actions to speak louder than my skin color and fight for the ideal "justice for all." I believe it can happen once more whites acknowledge the injustices people of color experience every day, mostly at the hands of whites, and work together openly and honestly to right these wrongs. Furthermore, I believe education and social awareness are the platforms in which this change has the chance to occur.

I think that being white is seen as a very negative attribute. I have had Black colleagues tell me, "Girl, you know you Black!" I laugh and know that this is meant as a compliment, and I am grateful that my Black colleagues think enough of me to pay me such a compliment, but facts are facts. I'm white. More importantly, I'm not ashamed to be white. I didn't choose my skin color and I didn't choose my parents, who failed me in every way imaginable. However, I can choose how I live my life, my values, and my purpose as that makes all the difference in how I impact others. I feel that my ability to teach has less to do with my race, as I consider myself a very capable woman.

However, I can be capable but ineffective if I don't connect to my students. Anyone can learn the curriculum, and instruction develops over time, but the impact is different. So being white makes me have to work harder to gain trust and connection, but that's okay because the results are worth it!

Lily Allison: At Killissac, I think I had to prove myself and show parents, students, and staff that I was there for the right reasons. I also had a lot to learn about teaching from an African lens. There were many things I didn't know and needed to research or ask questions about in order to really understand where the mission of the school came from. Being white at Killissac definitely impacted my relationship at first with many people. I think people didn't think I'd be able to relate to the school population and, to a certain extent, they were correct because I came from a very different background; however even though I couldn't relate, I could seek to understand and I think that was appreciated.

Q: In your opinion, how have you been able to be an effective teacher in an urban school setting for so long? Please explain.

Elizabeth DiFranco: It comes back to living a honest life. For good or bad, honesty is the best policy. Children, especially my students, can spot a phony when they see one. My kids have such a high social intelligence and vigilant character meter, that I must really walk the walk beyond talk the talk. I am a firm believer that actions speak louder than words and I believe my students are ever watchful of my actions. So far, I've passed the test.

I value my students and they know it. I believe in their abilities and talents and they know it. Most importantly, my kids have as much, or in many cases, more talent than their white counterparts, and I make damn sure they know it. I'm not about pity or victimization in any form. My goal is to support victors of success, not victims of a broken system.

High expectations, culturally relevant curriculum material, differentiated instruction, and lots of determination mixed with some honest, tough love. These elements are my strategic approaches as a teacher.

Lily Allison: Relationships first. I think that I have made it my mission working in urban schools to build those relationships with students and parents so that they trust me to do what's right by their children. I also strongly believe in all students' abilities to learn and I am constantly pushing them. I think it also helps that I have surrounded myself with like-minded educators who are willing to share ideas and strategies.

My current school is very much a family. We, the staff, know many of our families on a personal level, give out our cell phone numbers, go to students' after-school activities such as baseball games or robotics competitions. I guess this goes back to building those relationships. My students and their families know I genuinely care about them and their progress and therefore, they buy into what and how I'm teaching.

Q: Do you believe that there is such a thing as a "white savior complex" in urban education? Please explain.
Elizabeth DiFranco: Oh my God YES! Truth be told - I hate that this exists. Black students don't need whites to save

them. Ridiculous! Black students or any individuals of color just need fair opportunity. Period. Level the playing field, acknowledge the crippling effects of white privilege, the injustices of the legal system and educational system, and offer equal job opportunities based on ability and not exclusion based on race. As I read my response, it seems simple, but I must admit I am a very simple, no-nonsense type person, where common sense, common decency, and respect reign supreme. Savior, thankfully, isn't part of my vocabulary.

Lily Allison: Yes, however, I think there are different categories. Sometimes there are those (me!) who take a job in an urban district and are naive to the cultural differences. This person may not think of themselves as the "white savior" but also naively assumes that the way he or she taught in the suburbs or a rural district will work within an urban context. This was my very first year teaching and it was awful! I didn't know what I was doing "wrong". Why were none of the things I learned in teaching school working? Throughout that year, I learned a lot and became a better teacher.

Then, there are the people who have the same experience I did and don't learn from it and still continue to think that their way of teaching is the only way and that's what's going to "save" our urban youth. And finally, there are programs such as Teach for America where I think the real "white savior complex" lies. These programs seemingly say those working in urban schools don't know what they're doing so come join our program, we'll teach you everything you need to know in six weeks and then you'll be qualified to teach and turn our city schools around." I've only met one Teach for America graduate who has actually stayed in teaching and wasn't using it as something to pad their resume with. What our urban schools need are amazing teachers, no matter what color you are; who use culturally relevant pedagogy, and truly care about our kids. No saviors needed.

HOW DO YOU BECOME A CULTURALLY RESPONSIVE EDUCATOR?

The process of becoming a culturally responsive teacher is not really different from the steps you need to take in becoming a great teacher. Simply put, culturally responsive teaching is good teaching! If you are committed to placing your students in a position to be successful in life, you are a fan of culturally responsive teaching. If you are an educator who truly believes that all students have the ability to learn, then you are a fan of culturally responsive teaching.

When people hear the term 'culturally responsive teaching', they think of it as this foreign concept that is new to the world of education. Actually, it is a concept that has been in education for many years. The main reason why it is such a big deal now is because there is a greater emphasis on race and culture in America.

Considering the fact that a large population of students of color are personally impacted by controversial issues such as immigration, police violence, and mass incarceration, it is necessary for the modern-day educator to exercise cultural sensitivity when educating their students. In American public schools, our classrooms are becoming more culturally diverse. For that reason, we need to create learning environments that are engaging and accessible to all students. Below are the four steps that you can take in becoming a culturally responsive educator:

1. Evaluate Your Behavior

The truth is we are all prejudice and biased by human nature. You must hold yourself accountable for addressing any preconceived notions you have about race, ethnicity, and culture. You have to understand how these notions reflect your actions and impact the manner in which you educate your students. This evaluation must be done at both the staff and student levels.

For white teachers, they must first acknowledge that they are people of privilege and have been afforded freedoms that people of color are still fighting to attain to this day. In order to come to this realization, they must engage in literary research to build a fundamental understanding of how World history has informed the ideologies they have acquired about race and cultural identity. Through this research, they will also notice that laws and policies such as the Thirteenth Amendment and Jim Crow have historically been the vehicle for systematically oppressing people of color and maintaining the status quo.

For teachers of color, we must note that we are not exempt from this self-evaluation process as a result of their race. We must analyze and challenge stereotypical beliefs they not only have about white people but other people of color. Like our white counterparts, we must conduct our own research and question our own biases. No one is above reproach as this evaluation process must be done by all people who are in direct contact with students.

For any school to move forward, school leaders must create structured opportunities for staff members to have honest, transparent dialogue about race and cultural identity. Book talks and restorative justice practices are two examples of methods that can be used to generate those conversations. Although this dialogue can potentially bring about feelings of anger, frustration, and denial, it is necessary to allow these feelings to manifest so that the staff, as a whole, can work together to unpack them. Understanding the context from which each staff member developed their perspectives is an integral step to having these open conversations. By making the commitment to confront your racial and cultural biases, you are committing to create a positive classroom environment that is culturally inclusive and welcoming to all students.

2. Get to know your students

As educators, culturally responsive teaching cannot take place if we don't take the time to learn about our students. At the beginning of the school year, we typically have students' complete diagnostic assessments to determine their learning levels and identify specific skills in which they need extra support academically. The beginning of the school year is also a perfect time to get to know your students and their families on a personal level. This can be done by having students complete a survey or questionnaire, which will help you learn about their cultural background, learning preferences, academic strengths, needs, and hobbies outside of school. Accessing this information will enable you to get a head start in building positive relationships with your students.

Home visits are another effective way to strengthen your relationships with your students. There are certain families that want to be more involved with their children's education but they are not able to visit the school to meet with teachers because of their limited access to transportation. In other situations, the parents have work schedules that make it difficult for them to report to the school for conferences and family engagement events. By visiting their homes, you are showing families that you are committed to building a healthy partnership with them. Within their homes, parents feel more comfortable opening up and sharing personal information about their child that they otherwise wouldn't share in a school setting.

Be mindful that some families do not feel comfortable having teachers in their homes. Before making a home visit, be sure to ask the family for permission to visit. You can do this by sending home a permission slip or making a phone call. However you decide to communicate, the most important thing is to clearly state your intentions for the visit. Families are generally receptive to you visiting their homes when they see that you are going the extra mile to support their children's education.

3. Adapt your instructional strategies

Once you have gathered personal and academic data on your students, you can then use the data to inform your instructional practices. Since each student has their own set of academic strengths and individual learning needs, you must design learning activities that not only aligns with each student's learning preferences but addresses the academic areas in which they need the most growth.

For instance, if you have an ESL (English As a Second Language) student in your class who is from Vietnam and speaks very limited English, a possible form of support for that student can be a Vietnamese-English dictionary that will enable him to access content and translate words into his native language. Visual aids such as sentence starters and anchor charts of pictures accompanied with Basic English words can also support the student as he builds his English proficiency.

Depending on the racial and cultural composition of students in your classroom, the strategies you use to differentiate your instruction will change. If you teach in an inclusion setting where you have students on an IEP or are ESL, you cannot expect all your students to achieve learning gains if you employ a "one shoe fits all" instructional approach. If you need support with differentiating your instruction, connect with the coordinators from your school's special education and ESL departments to learn how you can best accommodate your students' needs.

Sometimes, adapting your instruction means utilizing pedagogical methods that connects academic content to current events in the world. A perfect example of this is when E. Christiaan Summerhill was teaching a lesson on democracy and civic action to his ninth-grade students at English High School. In an effort to connect the lesson to real life events, Summerhill showed his students a video of himself participating in a protest with thousands of Boston residents to voice their outrage about a New York grand jury's failure to indict a white police officer in the 2014 choking death of Eric Garner, an unarmed Black man. During the protest, Summerhill, along with other protesters, was arrested even though he was peacefully demonstrating.

When parents of two students complained to the school administration about Summerhill showing the video, the administrators moved to excise him from his teaching position. In response to the news, many students were prepared to stage a walkout in support of him. Even though the walkout never happened, this is clear evidence that students achieved the main objective of Summerhill's lesson, which was to exercise their democratic rights to speak out against issues that are unjust. More importantly, he adapted his instruction in a culturally responsive manner by connecting the concept of civic action to police brutality, an issue that personally hit home with many of his Black and Latino students.

As you are developing lessons and assignments for your students, it is important to exercise cultural sensitivity. Although you may have the best of intentions, you may be presenting information that provides an imbalanced and inaccurate representation of your students' racial and cultural history. Natalia Cuadra-Saez, a high school history teacher in Boston, recalls the moment when she reached that epiphany:

"I had a very bright student ask me, 'Ms. Cuadra, why do we always learn about Black people as victims? Can we learn about Black people like kings and queens?' This student really challenged my thinking and my practice. She and other students made me realize that my well-intentioned practices around teaching the history of oppression in this country was having the unintended consequence of demoralizing students. It changed the way I picked and presented my content and it made me focus on how best to empower my students, not just present them with what I considered the 'truth' they needed to know."

In teaching her Black students the 'truth' about their history in America, Natalia realized that it was just as important to highlight the positive attributes of their history so they have a balanced and complete view of their existence in America. Exposing her students to the influential figures of Black history will help them instill a sense of cultural pride and empower them to carry out the legacies of those figures. Given that the process of adapting our instructional practices is a student-centered endeavor, it is imperative that students are actively involved in this process. Their constructive feedback will provide data that will inform the adjustments you need to make to your lessons and assignments.

4. Be inclusive of all cultures

When planning your lessons, think about content that reflects and affirms the cultural diversity of your students. In creating a positive classroom environment, the primary goal is for your students to feel welcome and safe to show pride in their cultural identities. Cultural inclusion also provides a chance for students to learn more about each others' personally. The first three steps I've mentioned are examples of creating a culturally inclusive environment. Another example of this is recognizing major holidays or events of the different cultural groups represented in your classroom.

SUMMARY

Although it is apparent that the 'white savior complex' exists in the American public school system, it is imperative to note that not every teacher of color has the best interest of students of color in mind. I've witnessed this notion enough times throughout my career. In this current political climate where people, in general, are hypersensitive about issues of race, we lose sight of the fact that there are many great teachers who are doing great work with students of color and they just so happen to be devoid of melanin. On a personal note, my good friend and mentor Sara Demoiny is a white woman and is one of the most incredible teachers I've ever been around. My favorite teacher growing up, Mrs. Brenda Martin was a white woman. She took a shy, emotionally fragile kid and made him realize that he was not limited by his special education label or the fact that he had an Individual Education Plan (IEP). It is mainly because of her that I dedicated my mind, body, and soul into this important work.

Finally, I firmly believe that "not all skin folk are kinfolk". When I say *kinfolk*, I'm referring to any educator, irrespective of race and ethnicity, who has a genuine and vested interest in positively enriching the minds of Black and brown students. I'm proud to say that I've been blessed throughout my career to have worked with a number of great teachers who are cut from that fabric. Although I agree with the notion that more teachers of color, particularly males, are needed to close the academic achievement gap in public schools, I feel that it is even more imperative for urban school districts to train teachers to have culturally responsive teaching skills so that they are equipped to engage with students of different racial and ethnic backgrounds.

KWAME SARFO-MENSAH

IDENTITY TALK
WITH AN EDUCATOR

———

Earlier in the book, I discussed how I have been fortunate to have been guided by so many influential educators throughout my teaching career. Sara Demoiny has had a major influence on my development as an educator. During my first two years at Russell Byers, she served as my mentor teacher while I was working as a teaching assistant in her classroom. Throughout her sixteen-year career as an educator, Sara has served as a middle school math, science, and social studies teacher during her time in Philadelphia and worked as a professor at her alma mater, Carson-Newman College, in her native Tennessee.

Currently, she is the Assistant Professor of Elementary Education at Auburn University in Alabama, where she is teaching her pre-service teachers how to effectively marry academic standards with culturally relevant content in order to increase student engagement in the classroom. In this interview, Sara describes her evolution as an educator and specifies how her early experiences as a white teacher in an urban school setting have helped to alter her overall perspective about teaching.

Q: Describe your earliest introduction to teaching. What type of work were you doing? What were your initial impressions?

A: I completed a traditional undergraduate teacher education program. Once I graduated, I moved from Tennessee to Philadelphia and began teaching in a public middle school within the district. In my first year I taught sixth, seventh, and eighth grade social studies. In my first year, I had many moments where I questioned what I was doing. I am a white woman who began teaching in a school with a Black student population. I had many problematic mindsets entering the classroom, but the main question that frustrated me was, "Why have my students not responded to me?" I felt like I was working so hard, trying to make class "fun" and it didn't seem to matter. I didn't feel like the students respected me. At this point, I can critique everything I was doing, but initially, I didn't understand.

Q: Who is/are your personal mentor(s) in the field of education? In what ways have they supported your growth as an educator?

A: I believe my mentors have changed over time. Salome Thomas-EL and Akosua Watts were instrumental in my development as a K-12 teacher. Mr. EL showed me what culturally relevant teaching looked like. He embodied the tenet of cultural caring, and it was amazing to see his impact on students. Akosua showed me how to teach. She challenged me to keep learning and, through seemingly random conversations, helped me to question my views of Black culture and community.

Q: How were you able to overcome being a white teacher at an urban school? And do you believe that being a white teacher impacts your ability to teach students of color as well as interact with staff members or parents?

A: Definitely, yes. I wish that we could have a Russell Byers reunion so we could all teach together again because I think we have all grown so much. I really saw some cool things happen and thought about how much more we could do together again. So I think my long story, in short, is I went to a small Christian Liberal Arts College in Tennessee to get my Bachelor's degree and then moved to Philadelphia with my husband at the time and started at Stoddard-Fleisher Middle School right away, teaching eighth grade students. And I just always joked and I don't know if I said this to you at the time that I watched the movie "Dangerous Minds".

I watched it one too many times and then walked in the first day and I just didn't understand why I was trying so hard, and kids were still saying things like "Fuck You!!" to my face. And so there such a disconnect between everything and the fact that in my undergraduate program, I could write a lesson plan without a problem and I can make a yearly unit plan without a problem and no one in my school was doing that. I could do all of those things but I was never asked to critically think about my identity as a white woman and analyze how that plays out in society as well as affects me teaching social studies particularly. That's what I was teaching there. I was completely ignorant and oblivious, which isn't excusable, but was what was happening.

And so I think at Russell Byers, people weren't using languages like white privilege, white savior complex, or culturally relevant pedagogy. However, I felt like there were so many different people who were demonstrating how to be culturally relevant that I could just model in the classroom. I remember a specific conversation with Akosua Watts about dialect and language. I just remember sitting in the hallway after school one day. I don't remember exactly the context of the conversation, but I remember walking away thinking about dialect and questioning why I thought my English is the right Standard English and the way in which they're speaking English isn't correct.

Who's making those determinations? Again, we weren't using all of the languages to talk about issues of race or issues of being culturally competent, but it was just in those kinds of conversations that I think I had some growth at the time. It was still not nearly the kind of growth that I had at this point which I regret because I can name off a zillion ways in which I messed up and hurt my own students. Not intentionally but I did.

I definitely did not have the knowledge, language, or reflection that was needed. So, in every way, I think my identity and my whiteness affects the way I see the world and the way the world treats me. I've written my story before but I definitely talked about myself as thinking I was a white savior going into the classroom to help and save the poor Black kids. This is what I was thinking in my mind and not saying from my mouth at the time. It was definitely what I was playing out and I think my whiteness allows that to stay subconscious if I want it to. So I think there's a ton that I've learned just by going back to school and reading so much more and researching that I would love to be back in Philly and try again.

I think in any setting, honestly, but particularly in schools where a predominant number of students are of color, there has to be that overt conversation happening continuously with a white teacher. I think there needs to be a space in professional learning communities to discuss this issue. I think it needs to be something that is natural where it just happens all the time so that it doesn't feel like people are walking on eggshells talking about race and people are acting really uncomfortable. It needs to be a constant conversation and I think particularly in the past four to five years in our country, how could it not be? How can people think that we live in a post-racial society? I mean, that's ridiculous. There's no way that you could even begin to say that.

It's my responsibility to do that kind of interrogation as well as the constant reflection of what I need to do personally. But also I think structurally at the school level and at the district level, I have to think about how I'm pushing a whitewashed curriculum. How am I pushing against discipline policies or whatever that is inherently racist?

Q: Describe a moment in your teaching career when you faced a major challenge. What specific lesson did you learn from that challenge and how did it help support your growth as an educator?

A: I have a vivid memory of meeting with a parent who accused me of not liking her child. She wanted her son moved out of my room, and she did not trust me. I was flabbergasted at the moment and sat in shock. I told the mother that I disagree with her, and the administration supported me. Although the support was somewhat validating at the moment, this experience has always bothered me. At this point, I can look back and recognize that the mother had experiences that would cause her not to trust white teachers, which I understand. I needed to reframe my perspective of the student's behavior, and I should have leaned in to listen to the parent and consider her perspective more.

Q: What does it mean to be a culturally responsive teacher? How do you demonstrate cultural responsiveness within your own teaching practices?
A: At this point, I teach pre-service teachers in a PWI (Predominantly White Institution) university. I feel like my mission as a teacher educator is to bring awareness to my mainly white, middle class, Christian pre-service teachers to issues of oppression and power in our society. I talk explicitly about race and systemic racism in our society and schools. I feel like it is important for me to challenge their ideas of color blindness and (hopefully) help them to recognize white supremacy and to begin challenging it in their lives.

This semester, I have my students reading a book of counter-narratives in U.S. history, and they meet in weekly literature circles to discuss it. We just went on a field trip to the National Memorial for Peace and Justice and the Legacy Museum in Montgomery, AL. The students spent a lot of time reflecting before and after this trip, and they began to make connections to white supremacy in the past to its presence today.

Q: Any advice you would like to share to help individuals develop their teaching identities?

A: I think it is important to consider what activism looks like outside of one's classroom. I believe activism is good teaching, and I believe we have to consider how to address systemic issues as teachers in addition to individual actions in our own classroom.

BOOK RECOMMENDATIONS

———

IT'S A KNOWN FACT that educators have the reputation of being lifelong learners. In order to stay true to that reputation, it is important for educators to read and engage in literature that will help improve their teaching practices and provide a sense of direction in their careers. Building your intellectual capacity is essential to your progression as an educator.

During my interview sessions with educators, I asked each of them to name a book that they would recommend to an aspiring teacher looking to develop their own teacher identity. Some of the selections they mentioned were books that I already possessed in my personal library but then there were other selections with which I wasn't familiar. This revelation inspired me to compile a list of must-read selections that every educator should have in order to jumpstart their careers.

Below are the book recommendations that were made by the many educators I interviewed during the book writing process:

INSPIRATION

- *Apples of Grace: 31 Days of Inspiration for the Educator* by Cortland Jones
- *The Courage to Teach* by Dr. Parker J. Palmer
- *The First Days of School* by Harry K. Wong and Rosemary T. Wong
- *Fish in a Tree* by Lynda Mullaly Hunt
- *Grit* by Angela Duckworth
- *I Choose To Stay: A Black Teacher Refuses to Desert the Inner City* by Salome Thomas-EL
- *The Immortality of Influence* by Salome Thomas-EL
- *Make the Impossible Possible* by Bill Strickland
- *Nothing Impossible* by Dr. Lorraine Monroe
- *The New Teacher Book: Finding Purpose, Balance, and Hope During Your First Years In the Classroom* by Terry Burant, Linda Christensen, Kelley Dawson Salas, Stephanie Walters
- *The Teacher 50: Critical Questions for Inspiring Classroom Excellence* by. Dr. Baruti Kafele
- *Why We Teach* by Sonia Nieto
- *Your Next Chapter: How to Turn the Page and Create the Life of Your Dreams* by Manny Scott
- *Teach Like a Pirate* by Dave Burgess

CULTURALLY RESPONSIVE PEDAGOGY

- *A Talk to Teachers* by James Baldwin
- *Beyond Heroes and Holidays* by Enid Lee
- *Can We Talk About Race?* by Beverly Daniel Tatum
- *Crossing Over to Canaan* by Dr. Gloria Ladson-Billings
- *Countering the Conspiracy to Destroy Black Boys Vol. 1-4* by Dr. Jawanza Kunjufu
- *Culturally Responsive Teaching & the Brain* by Zaretta Hammond
- *Educating Teachers for Diversity* by Jacqueline Jordan Irvine
- *For White Folks Who Teach In the Hood…...and the Rest of Y'all Too….* by Christopher Emdin
- *MC Means Move the Class: The Elements of Urban Education* by Dr. Shaun Woodly
- *The Miseducation of the Negro* by Carter G. Woodson
- *Multiplication Is For White People: Raising Expectations for Other People's Children* by Lisa Delpit
- *Other People's Children* by Lisa Delpit
- *The New Jim Crow* by Michelle Alexander
- *Pedagogy of the Oppressed* by Paulo Freire
- *So You Want to Talk About Race* by Ijeoma Oluo
- *The Souls of Black Folk* by W.E.B. Du Bois
- *Why Are All the Black Kids Sitting Together In the Cafeteria?* by Beverly Daniel Tatum

EDUCATIONAL LEADERSHIP

- *Creating Connections for Better Schools* by Dr. Douglas J. Fiore
- *Eleven Rings: The Soul of Success* by Phil Jackson
- *Leading With Soul* by Lee G. Bolman and Terrence Deal
- *The Principal 50: Critical Leadership Questions for Inspiring Schoolwide Excellence* by Dr. Baruti Kafele

CHILD ADVOCACY& FAMILY ENGAGEMENT

- *The Importance of Being Little: What Young Children Really Need from Grownups* by Erica Christakis
- *Lost at School* by Dr. Ross W. Greene
- *Preparing Education to Involve Families* by Heather B. Weiss, Holly M. Kreider, M. Elena Lopez & Celina M. Chatman-Nelson
- *Reading for Their Life* by Alfred Tatum
- *Savage Inequalities* by Jonathan Kozol

ON-THE-JOB SITUATIONS

- *Difficult Conversations* by Douglas Stone, Bruce Patton, and Sheila Heen
- *Driven By Data* by Paul Bambrick-Santoyo
- *Who Moved My Cheese?* by Spencer Johnson

BIBLIOGRAPHY

"The 3 Questions to Help You Find Your Purpose." *Next Avenue*. Accessed October 19, 2018. https://www.nextavenue.org/3-questions-help-you-find-your-purpose/

"5 steps to becoming a culturally responsive teacher." *Teach Away*. Accessed October 14, 2018. https://www.teachaway.com/blog/5-steps-becoming-culturally-responsive-teacher

"7 Big Things You Should Understand About Teacher Pay, According To Teachers." *Money*. Accessed October 18, 2018. http://time.com/money/5387836/teacher-pay-big-misconceptions/

"8 Qualities of a Good Mentor." The Balance Careers. Accessed October 10, 2018. https://www.thebalancecareers.com/qualities-of-a-good-mentor-1986663

"About Us." Heart 2 Heart Services. Accessed September 25, 2018. https://www.hearttoheartservices.com/about-us

"Are You a Visionary or an Opportunist". Seth Sandler. Accessed October 8, 2018. http://sethsandler.com/leadership/visionary-opportunist/

"Black Lives Matter Demonstrators Cleared of Disorderly Conduct, Trespassing Charges." American Civil Liberties Union. Accessed October 14, 2018. https://www.aclu.org/news/Black-lives-matter-demonstrators-cleared-disorderly-conduct-trespassing-charges

"Boston teacher says dismissal tied to arrest in protest." Boston Globe. Accessed October 14, 2018. https://www.bostonglobe.com/metro/2015/06/22/teacher-reassigned-after-being-arrested-protest-against-police-violence/Q66IO3TmpEYfZhsyM7FYWJ/story.html

"Cultural Competence in Health Care: Is It Important for People With Chronic Conditions? *Georgetown.edu.* Accessed July 27, 2018. https://www.hhs.gov/ash/oah/resources-and-training/tpp-and-paf-resources/cultural-competence/index.html

DeAngelis, Toni. "In search of cultural competence." *American Psychological Association.* Accessed July 27, 2018. https://www.hhs.gov/ash/oah/resources-and-training/tpp-and-paf-resources/cultural-competence/index.html

"Delta Research and Educational Foundation Selects Project Director for Teacher Efficacy Program." *Delta Research and Educational Foundation.* Accessed September 25, 2018 http://www.deltafoundation.net/news-events/news/delta-research-and-educational-foundation-selects-project-director-for-teacher-efficacy-program

"Every Teacher Needs a Mentor." *Edutopia.* Accessed October 7, 2018. https://www.edutopia.org/article/every-teacher-needs-mentor

"Greenfield teacher wins national award for sharing personal story." *The Greenfield Recorder.* Accessed September 22, 2018. https://www.recorder.com/Greenfield-teacher-win-national-award-for-her-story-on-why-she-got-into-teaching-13322356

Hirsch, E.D. *Cultural Literacy: What Every American Needs to Know.* Boston, Houghton Mifflin, 1987.

"More than 300 TPS teachers resigning amidst contract renewal deadline." *ktul.com.* Accessed October 7, 2018. https://ktul.com/news/local/more-than-300-tps-teachers-resigning-amidst-contract-renewal-deadline

"Our Impact." *The New Teacher Center.* Accessed October 7, 2018. https://newteachercenter.org/our-impact/

"Social-emotional interventions are especially key to academic success, experts say." Education Dive. Accessed October 8, 2018. https://www.educationdive.com/news/for-special-needs-students-focus-on-sel-critical/427401/

"Some Oklahoma teachers find the grass is really greener in Texas." *Reuters.* Accessed October 7, 2018. https://www.reuters.com/article/us-oklahoma-education-exodus/some-oklahoma-teachers-find-the-grass-really-is-greener-in-texas-idUSKCN1HC136

"Student Trauma Is Widespread. Schools Don't Have to Go It Alone." *Education Week.* Accessed October 8, 2018. https://www.edweek.org/ew/articles/2018/02/26/student-trauma-is-widespread-schools-dont-have-to-go-alone.html

"Teachers Need a Growth Mindset Too." *Edutopia.* Accessed October 8, 2018. https://www.edutopia.org/article/teachers-need-growth-mindset-christina-gil

"Tell BPS to Apologize to Christiaan Summerhill." Move On. Accessed October 14, 2018. https://petitions.moveon.org/sign/tell-bps-to-create-a.fb50?source=s.icn.fb&r_by=13208578

"What 'white folks who teach in the hood' get wrong about education." PBS News Hour. Accessed October 7, 2018. https://www.pbs.org/newshour/education/what-white-folks-who-teach-in-the-hood-get-wrong-about-education

"Why Cultural Competence?" *National Education Association.* Accessed July 26, 2018. http://www.nea.org/home/39783.htm/

ACKNOWLEDGEMENTS

Thank you to my mother, Dorothy A. Mensah, for being my first teacher and helping me to believe that all things are possible if I believe in myself.

Thank you to my father, Sarfo Mensah Sr., for pushing me to be my own man and exposing me to the dos and don'ts of fatherhood.

Thank you to my brother, Sarfo K. Mensah Jr. and my sisters Abena and Konadu Sarfo-Mensah, for being the best siblings ever! Your support throughout my career and in life has been tremendous! Love you all!

Thank you to my lovely wife, Natalie Gill-Mensah, for being my partner in love and in parenthood. You have always pushed me to be the best version of myself and I appreciate you for continuing to stand by my side through thick and thin. I love you with all my heart!

Thank you to my son, Thaddeus Sarfo-Mensah, for giving me the honor of being your father and providing me with a fresh perspective on life. It is because of you that I gathered up the strength and courage to write this book. Keep shining, my son! Love you!

Thank you to my mother and father-in-law, Amelia and Garfield Gill, for taking care of Thaddeus and giving me the extra hours to work on this book. From day one, you have always been there for me and there aren't enough words to properly express the amount of gratitude I have for you. I love you both.

Thank you to Christie Lindor and Dolores Johnson for taking the time to impart their knowledge about writing. Your vote of confidence means everything, and I am forever grateful for your inspiring words.

Finally, I would like to thank every person who has made a valuable contribution to the making of this book. There are too many of you to name individually so just know that I am incredibly thankful for your support. God placed each of you in my life for a specific reason and I am thankful for your presence. It is because of you all that this book made it to the finish line. I am forever indebted to you.

30280410R00097

Made in the USA
Middletown, DE
24 December 2018